"During the past century, Pentec
of the tracks' movement to the most influential reality in global Christianity. And Vinson Synan has seen much of it happen firsthand. This is not only a wonderfully balanced account of the stages along the way—tent meetings, the Catholic charismatic renewal, televangelists, the Third Wave, the Toronto Blessing and much more—but a deeply moving account of a life that has been continually blessed by the Holy Spirit's surprises."

—**Richard J. Mouw**, president and professor of Christian philosophy, Fuller Theological Seminary; www.netbloghost.com/mouw

"In his book *An Eyewitness Remembers the Century of the Holy Spirit*, Vinson Synan shares the view from his front row seat for much of the work of the Holy Spirit in modern times. With the eye of an historian and the passion of a preacher, he details and critiques the major events of the Pentecostal past, both the profound and the problematic. It is a visionary and ecumenically sensitive memoir that gives great hope for the future of the Church and the world."

—**Kevin Ranaghan**, Ph.D., co-author, *Catholic Pentecostals*; co-founder, People of Praise

"In this book Dr. Vinson Synan gives evidence of why he is the dean of Pentecostal/charismatic church historians! From his personal perspective as a classical Pentecostal, he provides invaluable candid, colorful and perceptive insights and observations into the fruit of the Azusa Street revival as manifested through the faceted lens of twentieth-century personalities and events. Dr. Synan's warm, user-friendly style, along with his ability to provide the smallest details bristling with significance, make the reader feel personally involved in taking this Pentecostal journey all the way from Azusa Street to the twenty-first century. This is a must-read for every person desirous of identifying with his or her Pentecostal roots and pedigree."

—**Dr. Ronald W. Carpenter Sr.**, presiding bishop, International Pentecostal Holiness Church

"Dr. Vinson Synan has not only been an eyewitness from a strategic position to the Pentecostal movement during the past century; he has been deeply involved as a participant in the global expansion of the Gospel through those who have proclaimed that, as much as possible, the belief and practice of today's Church should mirror that of the early Church. You will find his reflections and observations informative and inspiring."

—**Dr. George O. Wood**, general superintendent, The General Council of the Assemblies of God

"Vinson Synan has been such an asset to the global Pentecostal community! His memories will define the pathway he followed so that others can walk in his footsteps, and all can receive an impartation of his vast knowledge and wisdom."

—**Bishop Charles E. Blake Sr.**, presiding bishop (seventh in succession), The Church of God in Christ

"*An Eyewitness Remembers the Century of the Holy Spirit* fascinates me. From its beginnings, the Pentecostal movement has validated the apostolic reality of its claim to the baptism with the Holy Spirit by one outstanding feature: its evangelism. The movement possesses a driving instinct to fulfill the Great Commission. It is my greatest honor to have had and still have a little part in that. I highly recommend this book."

—**Reinhard Bonnke**, D.D., international evangelist

"Vinson Synan is a towering figure in the charismatic renewal. He is a faithful historian of the worldwide move of the Holy Spirit. I know that *An Eyewitness Remembers the Century of the Holy Spirit* will inspire those who read it and motivate them to a deeper walk with the Lord."

—**Dr. Pat Robertson**, chairman, The Christian Broadcasting Network; president, Regent University

"A delightful and perceptive journey through a century of controversy and incredible growth in the Pentecostal/charismatic Christian subculture, this book is filled with personal vignettes and informative interpretations. As both participant and historian, Vinson Synan is uniquely qualified to tell this fascinating story."

—**David Edwin Harrell Jr.**, Daniel Breeden Eminent Scholar in the Humanities, emeritus, Auburn University

"For anyone who lived through the exciting days of charismatic renewal, this is a must-read history. Dr. Synan is not only an accomplished historian, but, as one of its great leaders, he took part at the highest level, and he shares with us the inner dynamics and inspiration of the renewal. In reading, I returned to the many dreams (and realities) of those glorious days."

—**Francis MacNutt, Ph.D.**, co-founder, Christian Healing Ministries

AN EYEWITNESS REMEMBERS THE CENTURY OF THE HOLY SPIRIT

VINSON SYNAN

Chosen
a division of Baker Publishing Group
Grand Rapids, Michigan

Published by Chosen Books
a division of Baker Publishing Group
P.O. Box 6287, Grand Rapids, MI 49516-6287
www.chosenbooks.com

Printed in the United States of America

ISBN 978-0-8007-9512-2 (pbk.)

Library of Congress Cataloging-in-Publication Data

Synan, Vinson.
An eyewitness remembers the century of the Holy Spirit / Vinson Synan.
p. cm.
Includes bibliographical references.
ISBN 978-0-8007-9485-9 (cloth)
1. Pentecostalism—History. I. Title.
BR1644.S95 2010
270.8′2—dc22 2009042011

10 11 12 13 14 15 16 7 6 5 4 3 2 1

I dedicate this book to all my history students over the years.

Among these are the first graduates of the Ph.D. program in Renewal Studies at the Regent University School of Divinity.

They are: David Moore, Eric Newburg, Charles Fox, John Miller and Matthew Tallman.

Contents

Foreword by Jack Hayford 9

Introduction 15

1. A Child of Azusa Street 19
2. The Latter Rain and Healing Revivals 31
3. Protestant Neo-Pentecostals 53
4. Catholic Charismatics 63
5. Charismatic Concerns and Controversies 77
6. New Orleans 95
7. The Prosperity Gospel 113
8. The Third Wave 127
9. Racial Reconciliation 141
10. Toronto, Brownsville and Lakeland Revivals 155

11. The New Apostolic Reformation Movement 171

12. Things I Never Expected to See in My Lifetime 187

Notes 207

Bibliography 212

Index 218

Foreword

You hold in your hand the reflections of one man—his life, his times and the remarkable nature of the season in Christian history that he has traversed. As reflections, they mirror more than thoughts and happenings; they reflect the life of a leader—one who moved through an extended awakening of the Holy Spirit's global working in the Church at large. As a Christian and an historian, Vinson Synan experienced and recorded what he witnessed; but more profoundly, he dramatically influenced significant aspects of what was occurring.

These facts alone would make this book worth reading. But beyond that, I want to relate why I am so grateful to be invited to write this foreword. It has more to do with the content of Vinson Synan's character than it does the remarkable nature of his influence.

I share a common heritage with Vinson in the historic classical Pentecostal movement, which heightens my respect for the price of his achievements far more than just recognizing the sum of them. God truly called Vinson Synan to a mission—one that is not yet over—that has led him to significant academic achievements and recognition. But in taking his place as a scholar, he risked ridicule by never removing himself from clear identification with the traditions of his family's Pentecostal faith heritage.

When Vinson earned his Ph.D. at the University of Georgia, many people still looked down on Pentecostals as uneducated and overly emotional folk. It would have been easy for him to distance himself from a movement perceived by many as far from sophisticated and even hostile to higher education. But Vinson was grateful for his heritage and set out on a career through which he would help bring new credibility to the unprecedented work of the Holy Spirit in the twentieth century.

Vinson Synan's life, expressed in these pages, demonstrates what Jesus called us all to be: salt and light (see Matthew 5:13–16). Not salt that stings the tongue and forces a decision to either spit or swallow, but salt that, by its capacity to introduce buoyancy to a chemical mix, lifts. Vinson lifted in love and service, and as a result brought great benefit that has accrued to all the Body of Christ. He also has been light, not to search out and embarrass, but to warm and attract many to God's work in our world. In so doing he has made his Pentecostal heritage stand out as a vital part of the Christian story that brightens the whole family of God.

This memoir reveals a man who has been a model for others to follow. What a remarkable and multidimensional life Vinson Synan has lived! He is a scholar and a proven leader as both an educator and an administrator. He has had a noteworthy journey as an ecumenist, participating in and leading events that have brought together Christians of all traditions under the banner of the Holy Spirit's renewing work. He has served as an evangelist and church planter and made significant contributions as a denominational executive in the Pentecostal Holiness Church.

But that is not what I want to highlight. I want to talk about the effect of Vinson's life as a humble believer in Christ, his experience as a committed Pentecostal/charismatic and his pursuits as a servant of Jesus' Church. To do so, I want to consider a familiar passage of Scripture and apply it to Vinson's life. It is the classic passage of Jesus in the Upper Room the night before the crucifixion:

> Now before the feast of the Passover, when Jesus knew that His hour had come and that He should depart from this world to the Father, having loved His own who were in the world, He loved them to the end. And supper being ended, the devil having already put it into the heart of Judas Iscariot, Simon's son, to betray Him, Jesus, knowing that the Father had given all things into His hands, and that He had come from God and was going to God, rose from supper and laid aside His garments, took a towel and girded Himself. After that, He poured water into a basin and began to wash the disciples' feet.
>
> John 13:1–5, NKJV

Not only is this passage a striking expression of humility, but it marks a prophetic moment of which Jesus was keenly aware. The phrase *His hour had come* makes clear Jesus' recognition that He was living out the purposes of God in which His obedience to the Father's will was crucial. These were not haphazard events, but part of God's redemptive plan.

Just as surely, God calls His children, redeemed by the life and work of His Son, to be coworkers with Him in His ongoing work in human history. Vinson Synan's life speaks to this reality.

When, a few years ago, I read of Vinson's participation in the 1972 conference at Notre Dame, at which he watched thousands of Catholic charismatics worship God, singing in spiritual language, I was deeply moved. I wept when I read of his weeping at Notre Dame, when he went aside from the meeting where he had just watched people whom his Pentecostal heritage had taught him to suspect expressing their passionate love for God.

I should point out that my own Pentecostal heritage contributed to a similar hesitance in me, at first, to affirm the Holy Spirit's renewing work among our Catholic brothers and sisters. We are all susceptible to our own blindness and undiagnosed prejudice.

Vinson was an example to Pentecostals and evangelicals alike of a humility that brought both tears and an open heart that embraced the work of the Spirit in his brothers and sisters in Christ. His openness was born out of a childlike simplicity that makes a person open and responsive to repentance and transformation. That moment in Notre Dame was the prophetic move of the Holy Spirit that occasioned Vinson's opportunity to lead the Church into new expressions of the unity Jesus prayed for in John 17:21.

In his efforts to bring together the various Christian traditions, Vinson had to risk misunderstanding and ridicule from his peers as he began to write about what God was doing among Catholics and mainline Protestants. The decades that have passed since then have helped erase the lines that divided various Christian groups. In that season of frequent sectarianism, Vinson fearlessly displayed an openness to the Holy Spirit, who constantly does new things in the Church. Those moments are never static; they are always in progress. And Vinson led the way with a true integrity of responsiveness to God.

This openness, like that of Jesus as He prepared to wash His disciples' feet, calls us to lay our own garments aside—the garments of self-respect and especially the garments of our own traditions when they divide us from other Christians, not to spite those traditions but to risk being misunderstood by those within them.

Vinson did so in reporting his 1972 Notre Dame experience at the Pentecostal Holiness Church's general conference the next year. At the time he wondered if he would be drummed out of the corps. Instead the convention elected him general secretary of the denomination. It was a tribute not only to his willingness to risk and lay aside his garments, but, perhaps more, to his commitment to recognizing God's prophetic moment.

Vinson Synan has demonstrated the humility of "laying aside his garments" in another significant way. Not only do denominations sometimes require a certain conformity, but so does the academic community. I say that not as a critique but as a simple fact of life. Although Vinson Synan's excellence in scholarship is widely recognized, he has written some of his books for more popular exposure and distribution. As a result he has borne a certain amount of criticism for being a popular or "folk" historian. In so doing, however, he has made his scholarship more accessible and has broadened the horizons of the Spirit's work to multiplied thousands. It is another of the risks Vinson has taken that has enriched all of us who have benefitted from his research and skillful writing.

Considering again John 13, I conclude with these words in mind: He "began to wash his disciples' feet." Vinson has been an interpreter for certain parts of the Body of Christ to other parts of the Body of Christ. He has done this not just for his own circle of classical Pentecostals but also for the rest of the Christian community, from Catholics to Calvinists. In this interpretive, integrating aspect of his life, I have never heard him speak lovelessly or unkindly about anyone or any tradition. He has helped the Church see and navigate the currents of God's renewing work and provided navigational aids without ever supposing he owned the charts. He has helped us "hear what the Spirit is saying to the churches." Along the way Vinson has modeled the humility and love Jesus demonstrated in washing the feet of the disciples, a group of very human men who were soon to deny, desert and even betray Him. Jesus served them anyway, loving His disciples to the very end.

Following his Savior, Vinson has loved the Church of Jesus Christ in deed and truth, participating in and chronicling marvelously "the century of the Holy Spirit." Vinson has helped us all realize Jesus' fundamental objective in John 13: "As I have loved you, that you also love one another" (NKJV). In the process he has gained much appreciation and forged many friendships. I count it an honor to be one of those friends.

Jack W. Hayford, founding pastor, The Church On The Way (Van Nuys, California)
Chancellor, The King's College and Seminary

Introduction

I've known Jane Campbell for many years. Often, she has talked with me about writing something for Chosen Books. When I told her that I was working on my autobiography, she wanted to see a copy. It soon became clear that she wanted a memoir rather than a detailed autobiography. Over the years, the idea of this book took shape. Most of our conversations took place at meetings of the Charismatic Concerns Committee, which met in Glencoe, Missouri. Jane is the person most responsible for the appearance of this book.

As we discussed the project, we agreed that the chapters would center around great events that I was involved in and include my personal comments about them. So the book would be a mixture of history and personal memoirs. Some chapters contain historical events that I've never written about before, but mostly the book is about well-known events that I've covered in previous books.

Of course, because I was born in 1934, I wasn't living during the entire century of the Holy Spirit. But I did live during two-thirds of the twentieth century and I'm still living in the first decade of the twenty-first century. My earliest memories were centered around life in my denomination, the Pentecostal Holiness Church. My exposure to the wider global Pentecostal world began in 1958 when I attended the World Pentecostal Conference in Toronto. I then became a historian of the movement with the publication of my University of Georgia Ph.D. dissertation, *Holiness Pentecostal Movement in the United States*, which appeared in 1971. My involvement in the broader Protestant charismatic world began in 1970 when I attended my first Full Gospel Business Men's Fellowship International convention in Charlotte, North Carolina. This was followed by my first introduction to the Catholic charismatic world at Notre Dame University in 1972.

In writing a book of memoirs, it's impossible to include every important person and event that deeply influenced my life. I could tell hundreds of stories about wonderful people I've known and exotic ministry trips around the world. But I eventually had to draw lines and boundaries in order to write a concise narrative. At least I've covered the highlights of my life and ministry.

Many individuals made it possible for me to write this book. My wife and chief editor, Carol Lee, edited every word before anyone else saw the manuscript. She is a wonderful helpmeet in all I have done. I also thank Jane Campbell for her inspiration and hard work at every stage of producing the book. Her suggestions and editorial work were crucial to its success. Others who have offered suggestions are David Moore, Father Timothy Cremeens and my twin brother, Vernon. I am also indebted to Brad Lewis for his editorial suggestions that vastly improved the final product.

So, for all it may be worth, here is my eyewitness account of some of the most important events in recent Church history—or more formally: *An Eyewitness Remembers the Century of the Holy Spirit.* To say the least, it has been exciting to meet so many thousands of wonderful people, to minister in so many nations and to play a small role in what I believe is the greatest spiritual and evangelistic revival in the last one thousand years.

Vinson Synan
Chesapeake, Virginia
August 2009

1

A Child of Azusa Street

I grew up in Virginia, where I took an early interest in history—especially American and Virginia history. As a child, I found American Civil War "minnie balls" (rifle bullets) almost everywhere as I worked in the vegetable patches my father planted before leaving for his summer rounds of camp meetings and conferences. When we moved to Chester, Virginia, our house was between the Confederate and Union breastworks. In grammar school, my teachers impressed upon me that the United States joined Virginia to form our nation.

My interest in history soon turned to the story of the church where I was born and raised. When I asked the old folks where the church came from, they answered, "From the Methodists." They always added that we were the oldest Pentecostal church, but not the largest.

I remember the day I asked my father who founded the Pentecostal movement. His answer was surprising and a little shocking for a twelve-year-old boy. He said it began in Los

Angeles, California, by a black man, William Seymour, who he said was a "one-legged man." (Later, I learned that Seymour had two legs but just one good eye, the other being blinded by smallpox.) Interestingly, my father didn't seem to know anything about Charles Fox Parham of Topeka, Kansas, who was the original proponent of speaking in tongues as the "Bible evidence" of the baptism in the Holy Spirit. It seemed inconceivable that a black man had been a founder of our church, which in my experience was made up almost entirely of whites.

Many years later, I also learned that the Pentecostal Holiness Church was a direct heir of the Azusa Street Revival. This occurred through Gaston Barnabas Cashwell, a North Carolina minister who traveled to Azusa Street in 1906 in search of his "personal Pentecost." After overcoming his racial prejudice, he allowed black hands to be laid on his blond-haired, blue-eyed head, after which Cashwell spoke in tongues. After returning to his hometown of Dunn, North Carolina, in January 1907, he led a historic revival that became known as "Azusa Street East." Hundreds of preachers and laymen from all over the South received the tongues-attested Spirit baptism. Lonnie and Hattie Edge, the preachers who led my father into the Pentecostal movement, were from the same North Carolina Conference of Cashwell's church.

As I went into high school and college, I became obsessed with a desire to learn more about the roots of the movement. How did Methodists become "Holiness"? How did sanctified people come to speak in tongues? Over time, I found that I was a "child of Azusa Street" by heritage. Through the years, I also learned much more about the Azusa Street Revival and how it launched Pentecostalism onto the global scene.[1]

What Happened at Azusa Street?

Christianity was forever changed by the Azusa Street Revival in Los Angeles at the beginning of the last century. Led by an African American pastor, William J. Seymour, the meetings were held in a run-down mission in downtown Los Angeles under the name "Apostolic Faith." During the height of Azusa Street's glory days, which lasted from 1906 to 1909, services were held three times a day, seven days a week for more than three years. While it seemed unlikely at the time, the Azusa Street Revival would serve as a major turning point in world Christian history.

The message that attracted multitudes to the Azusa Street mission was novel and revolutionary. Essentially, the new message proclaimed that modern Christians could receive a baptism in the Holy Spirit just as the apostles did on the Day of Pentecost. Speaking in tongues served as the "Bible evidence" of this Spirit baptism.

The theological father of this message was Charles Fox Parham, a former Methodist pastor who joined the Holiness movement. In the Bethel Bible School he founded in Topeka, Kansas, in 1898, his students affirmed that speaking in tongues provided evidence of the Pentecostal blessing. The first person to have this experience was Agnes Ozman. Her experience on the first day of the twentieth century became the prototype for modern Pentecostalism. In 1905, Parham became the mentor of William J. Seymour in Houston, Texas.

In 1906, Seymour brought the Pentecostal message to Los Angeles when he came to pastor a small black Holiness church. Although this church quickly rejected his message, Seymour began holding prayer meetings in a home on Bonnie Brae Street. As Seymour and several others spoke in tongues, they drew large crowds to the tiny house. After a search of downtown Los Angeles, Seymour and his flock found an old, abandoned African Methodist Episcopal church on Azusa Street. In April 1906, the historic Azusa Street services began.

Without question, the central figure at these meetings was Seymour. A somewhat mystical Baptist during his childhood in Louisiana, Seymour moved to Indianapolis as a young man. There, he joined a mostly white Methodist church, and later joined the Church of God (Anderson, Indiana), a Holiness group also known as the Evening Light Saints. Hungry for more biblical knowledge, Seymour attended classes at God's Bible School in Cincinnati led by Martin Wells Knapp, as well as Parham's Bethel Bible School in Houston, Texas.

Seymour was a soft-spoken pastor known in the black church as more of a teacher than a dynamic preacher. He was a deeply spiritual man who impressed other preachers who emerged from the wake of the Azusa Street meetings. William Durham said that he was "the meekest man I ever met," a man who maintained a "helpless dependence upon God" and "a man who is so filled with God that you feel the love and power every time you get near him." John G. Lake said of Seymour, "I do not believe that any man in modern times had a more wonderful deluge of God in his life than God gave that dear fellow, and the glory and power of a real Pentecost swept the world." As to his preaching style, Arthur Osterberg said he was "meek and plain spoken and no orator. He spoke the common language of the uneducated class. He might preach for three quarters of an hour with no more emotionalism than that there post. He was no arm-waving thunderer by any stretch of the imagination."[2]

The Legacy of Azusa Street

The most lasting and influential legacy of William Seymour and his Azusa Street meetings is the modern Pentecostal movement and its offspring, the charismatic movement. In many ways the Azusa Street mission serves as the prototype for modern Pentecostalism. Most of the religious world got news of the movement from Los Angeles rather than from Charles Fox Parham's leading in Topeka. The historical records show that the United States, Europe, Asia, Latin America and Africa all recognized that the new movement began in Los Angeles under a black pastor. Years later, leaders such as J. Roswell Flower drew attention to the roots of the movement led by Parham in Topeka.

The movement spread around the world under the ministries of the Azusa Street Pilgrims, preachers who received their Pentecostal experiences at Azusa Street. Among them were G. B. Cashwell (the American South), C. H. Mason (The Church of God in Christ), William H. Durham (Chicago, the American middle West and Canada), Mary Rumsey (Korea), A. H. Argue (Canada) and John G. Lake (South Africa). Later on, others indirectly influenced by Azusa Street took the Pentecostal message and experience around the world. These included Thomas Ball Barratt (Western Europe and Great Britain), Daniel Berg and Gunnar Vingren (Brazil), Willis Hoover (Chile), Luigi Francescon (Italy, Argentina and Brazil) and Ivan Voronaev (Russia and the Slavic nations).

The first Pentecostal denominations in the world were formed in the American South where Pentecostalism first gained a mass grassroots following. Most of these groups formed prior to 1900 as Holiness churches and saw the Pentecostal experience as a "third blessing," in addition to salvation and entire sanctification. These denominations included: the Church of God in Christ (Memphis, Tennessee), the Pentecostal Holiness Church (North Carolina), the Church of God (Cleveland, Tennessee), the United Holy Church (North Carolina) and the Pentecostal Free Will Baptist Church (North Carolina).

Beginning in 1914, American Pentecostal churches from non-Wesleyan backgrounds were formed. These included the Assemblies of God (Missouri), the Pentecostal Church of God (Missouri), the International Church of the Foursquare Gospel (California) and the Oneness denominations: the Pentecostal Assemblies of the World (Indiana) and the United Pentecostal Church (Missouri). Directly or indirectly, every classical Pentecostal movement around the world can trace its spiritual roots to the humble mission on Azusa Street. In this sense, the church I was born into was an outgrowth of the Azusa Street Revival. Therefore, as a Pentecostal, I was a "child of Azusa Street."[3]

My Azusa Street Experience

My first memories of Azusa Street–like Pentecostal worship were in the Suffolk, Virginia, church my family attended during the years of World War II. I vividly recall the sermons my father preached to the little congregation, which seldom numbered more than 75 people. As a preacher's kid, I was at church every time the doors were open. This often meant sleeping on blanket pallets under the pews as the Pentecostal worshipers shouted and danced around me in the aisles.

Other unforgettable impressions include the expressive and emotional worship of this little band of Pentecostal believers. Beginning with hearty shouts of "Amen" and "Hallelujah," the service usually moved to higher and louder levels as the meeting progressed. A major highlight was the "shout in the camp" when the preacher reached one of several oratorical climaxes in his sermon. At the end of the preacher's message, the "power would fall." People would be on their feet "shouting the victory" and dancing in the aisles. Others might fall out "slain" in the Spirit when they were "filled with the

Holy Ghost." Occasionally, people would speak in tongues or prophetic utterances. But tongues were sought and valued mainly as evidence of receiving "the baptism." The altar calls were a sight to behold and sometimes painful to hear. People crowded to the front of the church seeking salvation, sanctification, baptism in the Holy Spirit or divine healing. Often, the roar of concert prayer was deafening.

I also remember extended revivals that lasted two weeks to a month. In the days before air-conditioning, visiting evangelists preached graphic sermons on heaven and hell, the Second Coming and the rise of the Antichrist. During the altar calls for sinners to repent before it was too late, I often felt sorry for the sweating evangelists who begged for someone to come forward. To relieve their anxiety, I often raised my hand and went forward whether I needed to or not. At least the poor evangelists could count on one "conversion." In spite of my repeated responses to these altar calls, I clearly remember the day when my mother told me about Jesus and I accepted Him as Savior and Lord. Although I was just four years old, I remember being very happy that someday I would go to heaven.

One of the happiest times in any service came after the altar-call "breakthrough" when many people had received definite experiences from the Lord. The time of singing and rejoicing by the exhausted saints after the altar service represented a spiritual high point I've seldom seen since those days. Often, my father played the piano and led in singing "This Is Like Heaven to Me" and "The Old-Time Power" as worshipers rose to ever-higher levels of praise and rejoicing. Many of these people were poor in worldly goods, but extremely rich in spirituality and joy.

In Suffolk, I also witnessed one of the greatest healing miracles in my life. My father nearly died of typhoid fever, which he'd contracted after preaching in a camp meeting in Oklahoma. For many days, his fever raged at such a level that my siblings and I weren't allowed to enter his room. I remember the doctor giving us typhoid shots so painful that we could hardly raise our arms for days. At one point, the doctor despaired for my father's life. One day a preacher friend, Joseph Campbell Jr., felt led to come and pray for him. According to my father, Campbell "prayed for hours, all over the room, almost climbing the walls" in fervent petition. His voice could be heard all over the house. That very day, the fever broke and my father was completely healed. We were all thankful for the great healing that we saw with our own eyes.

At the end of World War II, my family moved to Hopewell, Virginia, the town where I'd been born a decade earlier. In Hopewell, our lives revolved around the church and schools we attended. In grammar school and high school, fellow students and even our teachers mocked us, calling us "holy rollers." Although the name of the church was "Pentecostal Holiness," we were universally known as the "Holiness Church." The word "Pentecostal" never seemed to stick.[4]

I was always puzzled that we were taught not to criticize Jews or Catholics because that would be bigotry or prejudice. And of course, no one dared to criticize the Baptists or Methodists because there were so many of them. Yet the teachers often led in the mockery and criticism of the Holiness people—even right to our faces.

Many revivals punctuated those years as leading evangelists came to preach in the Pentecostal style. I remember a calendar on the wall of my uncle's home with a photo of a young evangelist and his wife named Oral and Evelyn Roberts. In 1948, my father and Oral Roberts preached together in the Falcon Camp Meeting in North Carolina. No one would have guessed that the tall, dark and lanky Roberts would later become a household word and be the first of a new genre of preachers, the "televangelist."

Music in the church was lively indeed. The old Wesleyan and Holiness hymns were sung with great joy and much hand clapping. My uncle Lindsay was a "foot-stomping, leg-whopping" Pentecostal preacher. His sermons usually ended with the congregation rising to their feet and shouting or "running the aisles." When revivals reached a fever pitch of excitement, the altars would be jammed five people deep with people seeking for the "deeper experiences."

Preaching on the Second Coming of Christ—often called "the Rapture" by Pentecostals—accelerated after the proclamation of Israel as a state in 1948. Many preachers issued dire warnings about the end of the world and the pitiful plight of sinners who would be left behind after the sanctified few were caught away. I remember coming home from school one afternoon to find the house empty. Even my mother wasn't there. Chills went up and down my spine as I realized that the Rapture might have taken place. With all my shortcomings, I'd been left behind to face the Tribulation alone. I also remember the wonderful feeling when everyone returned home and I found that I hadn't been left behind.

Camp meetings held each summer at the grounds at Bermuda Hundred near Hopewell drew hundreds of worshipers. The youth camps provided opportunities for teenagers to "pray through" after engaging in mischief during the days. Usually, a sermon on the Rapture of the saints brought the youth to the altars for extended hours of prayer and seeking the Lord. The threat of the imminent Rapture was so intense that I never believed I'd live long enough to marry and have a family. I once heard my twin brother, Vernon, earnestly praying that Jesus would delay His return until he could get married. Years later, I teased him, saying, "After forty years of marriage you're now praying, 'Even so, come now, Lord Jesus.'"

I now realize that the basic message of the churches I attended while growing up was much more of a Wesleyan-Holiness nature than Pentecostal. Sometimes, Wesley was quoted more than the apostle Paul. Many preachers emphasized holy living as the ultimate goal, more than exercising spiritual gifts. In time, my father and Uncle Lindsay became warriors in defense of instant sanctification as a "second work of grace." Sermons bristled with denunciations of such perceived false teachings as "Finished Work," "Russellism" and "Jesus Only." Part of the Holiness ethos was simplicity of dress and separation from the world along with all forms of "worldliness." Of course, Holiness folk abstained from tobacco and alcohol—in fact, these filthy sins of the flesh were "forbidden" by the *Discipline of the Pentecostal Holiness Church*.

Restrictions certainly didn't end there. Women were not to "bob" or cut their hair, wear lipstick or wear immodest dress such as pants or pantsuits. Of course, cursing, swearing or using vulgar or suggestive language was forbidden. So were movies, the theater, fairs and other "worldly amusements." Church members who got caught indulging in any of these infractions were brought before the church and expelled if they refused to repent and change their ways.

While my home church abided by these "disciplines," it still grew to be one of the largest in town, eventually building a large sanctuary on a main street of the city. Probably very few people were aware of the Azusa Street spiritual roots of the church, because our church—which was mostly made up of white people—was rooted deeply in the post–Civil War white culture of the South. Despite the segregation of the times, however, we were the only church in town that had a black member. Also, in the tradition of Azusa Street, our church and the local Black Apostolic church conducted pastoral exchanges where we attended each other's churches at least once a year.

Azusa Street and the Whole Body of Christ

The little band of worshipers that gathered at Azusa Street in Los Angeles in 1906 never dreamed of the historic results of the revival they helped to unleash. They never belonged to a large denominational group. None of the large Pentecostal denominations of today, such as the Assemblies of God or the Church of God in Christ, can lay exclusive claim to the mission.

Azusa Street belongs to the whole Body of Christ. Seymour can't be claimed only by blacks or by Pentecostals. He belongs to the whole Body of Christ—of all nations, races and peoples. And the baptism in the Holy Spirit—with its accompanying gifts and graces—doesn't belong only to the Pentecostals. It belongs to the whole Body of Christ.

As I dig into the incredible story of Azusa Street, I now realize that the church I grew up in taught what theologians now call the "Fivefold Gospel." Seymour taught the same at Azusa Street, and it includes a new birth conversion, sanctification as a cleansing "second blessing" preparation for the baptism in the Holy Spirit, tongues as the "initial evidence" of baptism in the Holy Spirit, divine healing "as in the atonement" and the premillennial Second Coming "Rapture" of the sanctified Church.

Looking back, I also realize that my career stems from the Pentecostal movement unleashed in the humble Azusa Street Mission in Los Angeles. This includes a denominational career of planting four local congregations; serving as General Secretary and Assistant General Superintendent of the Pentecostal Holiness denomination; my education (M.A. and Ph.D. at the University of Georgia); my sixteen historical books including *The Holiness Pentecostal Movement* (1971) and *Century of the Holy Spirit* (2001); my academic career at Oral Roberts University and Regent University; and my part in the founding of the Society for Pentecostal Studies in 1970.

Indeed, I grew up as a "child of Azusa Street," but I had much more to learn about my Pentecostal heritage.

2

The Latter Rain and Healing Revivals

As I mentioned earlier, at the end of World War II our family moved back to Hopewell, Virginia, the city where I was born. We moved because my father had been elected as a bishop of the Pentecostal Holiness denomination, which involved long periods of travel by train all over the nation. In Hopewell, we lived near my uncle Lindsay, who was pastor of the local church that was located only a block from our new home. Our uncle could help with the task of governing our large family of seven children—five boys and two girls.

Most of my spiritual formation took place in Hopewell. The fast-growing church was a dynamic and very Pentecostal congregation, much noisier than the Suffolk church. Much shouting and even screaming took place during my uncle's passionate sermons. The incredible altar calls included scores of seekers lining the altars and seemingly obeying the Scripture "the violent take it by force" (Matthew 11:12).

My uncle invited the most effective evangelists to the church during the quarterly revivals that punctuated the church calendar. Among them were women evangelists such as Katie Campbell, Hattie Edge and several women "Evangelistic Parties" such as the Johnson-Houser and Gaskins-Faircloth parties. Katie Campbell defended her right to preach by repeatedly saying, "A woman brought sin into the world, so a woman should help take it out again."[1]

The most effective evangelist at the Hopewell church in the postwar period was a tall and handsome preacher from Oklahoma by the name of Oral Roberts. After leading successful revivals in the Hopewell church, he and my uncle Lindsay became fast friends. Between revivals, Uncle Lindsay would pay Roberts $5 a day to help him paint houses and hang wallpaper. This helped the impoverished evangelist survive between revival offerings that were often very small.

When we began to attend Hopewell High School, four of the five brothers played in the high school band. This was risky for the sons of a bishop, because the band played at all the football games. Hopewell dominated state football during those years, winning 35 straight games and three class AAA state championships. To some church people, my father was becoming a "liberal" by the Holiness standards of the day. On the other hand, my uncle was extremely conservative, especially on matters of dress for women. No lipstick, "needless ornamentation" or "bobbed hair" was the rule.

As we grew up, most of my siblings and cousins were very active in the music program of the church. Three Synans eventually became professional musicians and educators: my sister Maurine, my cousin Madeline and my twin brother Vernon.

During these years in Hopewell, I became more and more interested in what was happening in our Pentecostal subculture. I heard negative pulpit references to the "Finished Work," "Oneness" (or "Jesus Only") and "Latter Rain" movements that seemed to be threatening and dangerous—although I now admit that I had no idea what they were. In time, I learned that the Finished Work people had abandoned sanctification as a second blessing and were too worldly. I learned that the Assemblies of God were the leading proponents of this theology. The Oneness Pentecostals denied the Trinity and taught that they and they alone could be saved. Anyone who refused water baptism in "Jesus' name" would be lost. And finally, the Latter Rain people were hard to define. But I understood clearly that they were dangerous people with disturbing teachings and practices.

A Watershed Year

All of this came into focus in the historic year of 1948. In retrospect, this year served as one of the major turning points in American religious history. I remember the headlines that announced the formation of the State of Israel in May. For years afterward, almost every sermon I heard referred to the soon-coming Rapture of the Church, because of the belief that all of the biblical prophecies surrounding this event had been fulfilled.

Another major event occurred in August 1948 with the founding of the World Council of Churches (WCC). We were told that this organization represented the beginning of the liberal apostate church, which would help bring on the Tribulation and the reign of the Antichrist. The WCC was a renamed version of the liberal Federal Council of Churches that had existed since 1908. In 1950, the American-based National Council of Churches (NCC) was formed in Chicago.

In opposition to the Federal Council of Churches (and later the WCC), the National Association of Evangelicals (NAE) was formed in 1942. The main reason this new organization formed was to prevent the U.S. Congress from passing laws controlling religious broadcasting on radio and in the newly developing TV industry. Rumors spread that only government-approved programs would be permitted, and these would come only from mainline denominations. This would have knocked Charles Fuller off the air and made it impossible for future evangelists such as Billy Graham, Oral Roberts or Pat Robertson to buy airtime. Indeed, 1948 was the year that Graham and Roberts made their debuts on the national scene. Above all others, they created the genre of televangelist that dominated Christian broadcasting in the coming decades. In a surprising move, three American Pentecostal denominations joined the NAE in 1943: the Assemblies of God, the Pentecostal Holiness Church and the Open Bible Standard Churches. Other Pentecostal churches joined in following years. Russell Spittler calls this move the beginning of the "evangelicalization of Pentecostalism" in America.

For Pentecostals, 1948 was also a critical year. After being accepted by other evangelical denominations in forming the NAE, Pentecostal leaders were suddenly brought together in the same room after decades of separation. According to J. Roswell Flower of the Assemblies of God, early Pentecostals preached together and had rich fellowship before the divisions caused by the Finished Work and Oneness movements. After that, however, there was no contact at all for more than twenty years. In 1948, in Des Moines, Iowa, the Pentecostal Fellowship of North America (PFNA) was formed. In fact, my father represented the Pentecostal Holiness Church in creating the new group. Sadly, no African Americans were invited.

Even so, this was the first-ever ecumenical organization of American Pentecostals.

The Latter Rain Movement

The Latter Rain Movement, I learned much later, began in Canada at Sharon Bible College in North Battleford, Sasketchewan. This small, independent Pentecostal school had its roots in the Pentecostal Assemblies of Canada and the Church of the Foursquare Gospel. On February 12, 1948, a revival broke out among the students that spread rapidly across Canada and the United States. Leading the movement was George Hawtin and others who reported signs and wonders and renewed gifts of the Holy Spirit that individuals received with the laying on of hands. The revival also included people singing in tongues and the casting out of demons. The Pentecostal movement was at a low ebb in 1948, with a growing dryness and lack of charismatic gifts. Many who heard about the events in Canada believed that it was a new Azusa Street, with many healings, tongues and prophecies. A large center of the revival outside of Canada was the Bethesda Missionary Temple in Detroit, Michigan, pastored by Myrtle Beale. From Detroit, the movement spread across the United States like a prairie wildfire.[2]

Soon, opposition arose to this movement in the mainline Pentecostal denominations. Some accused people in the Latter Rain Movement of "conferring" specific gifts of the Spirit on individuals. A more troubling problem was the teaching that an end-time group of "super apostles," known as the "manifested sons," would usher in the end times and the Rapture of the Church with the Second Coming of Christ. Another emphasis was the restoration of what they called "the fivefold ministries" as listed in Ephesians 4:11. These were apostles, prophets, evangelists, pastors and teachers.

Perhaps the biggest problem was that the Pentecostal establishment felt threatened by the vigor and attractiveness of the new movement. In a short time, the Assemblies of God, the Church of God (Cleveland, Tennessee), and the Pentecostal Holiness Church rejected the Latter Rain Movement, although some aspects were resurrected in the charismatic movement after 1960.

A positive aspect of the Latter Rain Movement was a growing manifestation of the gifts of the Spirit in regular Pentecostal services. We witnessed less of this in the Pentecostal Holiness Churches than in other Pentecostal churches. For us, it was rare to hear a "message" in tongues with interpretation, and even rarer to hear a prophecy in the first person, as if God Himself were speaking. In fact, I once heard my father interrupt messages in tongues and prophecies that he thought were out of order. For many Holiness-Pentecostals, tongues was evidence of baptism in the Holy Spirit and little more.

Little David and Oral Roberts

My first introduction to the healing crusade ministry occurred after 1948 with the ministry of "Little David" Walker in Richmond, Virginia. Then a twelve-year-old boy, Little David packed the great Mosque auditorium in Richmond, which held several thousand people. Many of our friends in Hopewell joined the crowds to hear the child evangelist and were almost ecstatic about the healings they witnessed. Although these same people would never darken the door of our church, they flocked to the healing crusades.

I realized that the healing message had a wider potential audience outside the classical Pentecostal churches. Also in Richmond, the Calvary Pentecostal Camp Meeting was run by Wallace and Ruth Heflin. Most of the classical Pentecostal churches in the area opposed the Heflins mainly because of the abundant Latter Rain manifestations. Our people were forbidden to attend the Heflin camp meeting services.

By far, the biggest healing crusade ministry that I saw personally was the 1949 Oral Roberts crusade in Norfolk, Virginia. I'll never forget the conversations between my dad and Uncle Lindsay as we drove to the big tent. They marveled that this was "not the same Oral" they'd known through the years. They said I'd see the largest crowds I'd ever seen in my life. Indeed, more than three thousand people were present that night under the "Tent Cathedral." I couldn't imagine that a Pentecostal Holiness pastor from Oklahoma was now very famous. Even more impressive, *Life* magazine ran a story on Oral stating that he was from the Pentecostal Holiness Church. When the story ran, one of our bishops, T. A. Melton, proclaimed, "This is a dark day for the Pentecostal Holiness Church."[3] This attitude was very hard for me to understand.

Although our family had always loved Oral Roberts, my father began to have second thoughts about his ministry. He especially doubted Oral's claim to feel healing power in his right hand. Roberts's teachings on prosperity—fueled by his reading of Napoleon Hill's book, *Think and Grow Rich*—opened him up for special censure. Also, he seemed to be downplaying the experience of entire sanctification, which the Pentecostal Holiness Church had always held as a crucial cardinal doctrine. Probably the greatest problem arose, however, when my father and uncle took my grandmother Synan to Oral's crusade in Richmond in 1950 so he could pray over her for her advanced case of breast cancer. Some time after Oral pronounced her healed in a private prayer session, she died a horrible death. After this, the Synans were even less sure about Oral's ministry.

On the positive side, during that same crusade, I saw one of the greatest miracles in my life. A member of the Hopewell church, Mrs. Gatlin, was raised up from her wheelchair after Oral prayed for her. For years, we had seen her only on the first Sunday of the month when communion was served, and she always made her way to the altar in her wheelchair. The next Sunday after her healing, she walked into church. And she led a normal life for years after that.

Another miracle of Roberts's crusades was the joining together in prayer meetings and planning sessions of Pentecostal pastors who had rarely spoken to each other before. For the first time, pastors from the Assemblies of God, the Church of God and even the United Pentecostal Church laid aside their differences and joined in supporting the crusades. I'll never forget one Oneness pastor who played the accordion and sang with what seemed a normal amount of anointing. Although we were warned about his doctrinal errors, he was allowed to participate and even lead worship. For those days, this was a rare example of Pentecostal unity indeed.[4]

The Oneness question was also laid aside when William Branham came to Richmond a short time later. Most of the local Trinitarian Pentecostal churches supported him, even though he was a professed follower of the "Jesus Only" ("Oneness") movement. Although I didn't attend his Richmond meeting, I heard of fantastic healings and "words of knowledge" where Branham apparently read people's minds and made medical diagnoses on the spot. I also recall that Branham chided the Pentecostals of Richmond for having only seven hundred members in all their local churches combined.

The effect of the healing crusades on our local church was enormous. Soon, people who had attended the Walker,

Roberts and Branham crusades began to show up in church. Around 1950, the church doubled and tripled in attendance. Before long, the old sanctuary was far too small for the crowds of more than three hundred attending Sunday school, and the sanctuary was packed for each service. In 1953, work began on a new church building that seated seven hundred people. By then, I was a student at Emmanuel College in Georgia, but in the summertime, I hauled bricks, cinder blocks and mud for the bricklayers working on the massive building.

In the broader church, however, the healing crusade movement became the primary issue of debate for many years. Paul F. Beacham, president of Holmes Bible College in Greenville, South Carolina, became an outspoken critic of the whole movement. For at least a generation, students graduated from Holmes with stern warnings against the divine healers, and especially against Oral Roberts. At the same time, Oral had many supporters and employees on his staff from the Pentecostal Holiness Church. These included O. E. Sproull, Collins Steele, Lee Braxton, G. H. Montgomery, Bishop Oscar Moore, and in later years at Oral Roberts University, Dr. R. O. Corvin, Dr. Paul Chappell, Harold Paul, Dr. Carl Hamilton and myself.

The controversy in the Pentecostal Holiness Church over Roberts's ministry came to a boiling point in the 1953 General Conference, which met in Memphis, Tennessee. Due to pressure from his avid followers, Roberts was invited to be a main evening speaker. Delegates came from all over the United States ready to vote for or against his ministry. When Oral preached to a capacity crowd, the response was so overwhelmingly positive that the divisiveness evaporated. In an apparent bid for church support, Oral offered to give $50,000 to the Southwestern Pentecostal Holiness College in

Oklahoma City where he had once taught. Not only did the delegates accept the offer, they elected Roberts's close friend Oscar Moore as a bishop of the church.[5]

All of this was in the air when my brother Vernon and I enrolled at Emmanuel College in 1953. We had graduated as members of the honor society at Memphis Central High School, which was the second-highest ranked high school in the United States (second only to the famous Boston Latin Grammar School). We were well prepared for college and did very well in our classes. Our two years at Emmanuel were punctuated by the Roberts's controversy, because Roberts was extremely popular with most of the students, and our father's opposing views were well known.

While in college, I sang in a male quartet that traveled on recruiting trips for the school. We sang in scores of churches from Alabama to Virginia. On one trip, we happened to be in Florence, South Carolina, at the same time Oral Roberts was holding a mass healing crusade. We attended out of curiosity. The tent was overflowing with more on the outside than could get inside, with the crowds estimated at more than twenty thousand people. Interestingly for the times, Roberts refused to segregate blacks from whites, and this was the most integrated religious meeting I'd ever seen.

An important opportunity came in 1958 when some preacher friends convinced me to attend the World Pentecostal Conference with them. At this conference, which convened on the Fairgrounds in Toronto, Canada, I saw the strength of the worldwide Pentecostal movement for the first time. People from all over the world spoke of great growth and success in evangelism and church planting. One of the most impressive speakers was Nicolas Bhengu, a black Assemblies of God pastor with a huge church in South Africa. I had no idea that the movement was so large and influential. I determined to learn as much about the history of the movement as I possibly could.

Although the Toronto newspapers were merciless with negative articles and photos, the delegates left the conference with a sense of destiny. Much of the worldwide growth was fueled by the mass crusades of Roberts in the United States and by Tommy Lee Osborn, who brought the mass healing crusade ministry to the Third World. I remember that the Osborns sent their son, Tommy Jr., to Emmanuel Academy (high school) when he was barely a teenager. Even then, he was a guitar-playing rambunctious Pentecostal preacher. We often played the guitar together.

In time, the controversy over the healing crusade movement subsided as Oral Roberts's ministry grew to be larger than the Pentecostal Holiness denomination itself. When Oral Roberts University was dedicated in 1965, my father—who was still Oral's bishop—was asked to read the Scriptures. And Billy Graham gave the dedicatory message.

When I was a student at Emmanuel in 1955, I met Demos Shakarian and heard him speak. In the chapel service, he told about the founding of the Full Gospel Business Men's Fellowship International (FGBMFI) and his views on the baptism in the Holy Spirit and healing. But it was his prosperity testimonials that were the most unforgettable. His pilot said that he had once flown two hundred miles on an empty tank of gas. Shakarian wasn't an outstanding speaker, but we were impressed by the fact that he owned the largest dairy herd in the world and that he was reaching thousands of businessmen with the Pentecostal message—men who would probably never enter a Pentecostal church. Little could I have imagined that one day I'd have the privilege of interviewing Demos for sixteen hours and of publishing a history of FGBMFI titled *Under His Banner*.[6]

Academia

After graduating as salutatorian at Emmanuel College in 1955, I returned home to pursue my education at the nearby University of Richmond, a Baptist institution. I was treated well by the people there, especially by Dean Pinchbeck. I learned later that he was the famous "Dean Beck" in Earl Hamner's book *Spencer's Mountain*, which served as the inspiration for the TV series *The Waltons*.

I was somewhat of a curiosity at Richmond because I was only the second person from my denomination to ever enroll there. Although I primarily studied history, I took three courses in religion. I was totally shocked by the religion professors and their extremely liberal views. In fact, one class seemed to revolve around discussions of sexual perversions of which I'd been totally unaware. To graduate, students needed to take two years of two foreign languages. I took French and Spanish from the same teacher. Also, I wrote a bachelor's thesis to graduate in history. Indeed, this was great preparation for my M.A. and Ph.D. studies several years later.

While taking classes six days a week at Richmond, I accepted a call to pastor the Mount Olive Pentecostal Holiness Church near Fredericksburg, Virginia. While there for two years, the church grew and we finished a new sanctuary. During the next few years, I also helped plant and organize two other churches in Virginia, as well as a new church in Hartwell, Georgia. I was also often invited to conduct "youth revivals" in many churches.

As a single pastor, I was the target of many mothers who saw me as a good catch for marrying their daughters. I learned the truth of the old adage "It takes two to make a marriage—a girl and her mother." Often, the altars were full of weeping teenage girls whose mascara ran down their faces as they prayed for the "deeper experiences." All of this came to a sudden halt when I met the girl of my dreams at the camp meeting near Hopewell in 1958. She was Carol Lee Fuqua from the Richmond church. After two years, we were married and eventually were blessed with two daughters and two sons.

In 1959, I was called unexpectedly by Woodard Drum, president of Emmanuel College, who invited me to teach history because a teacher had left at mid-term. Sensing that this was of God, I resigned as president of the Pentecostal Holiness Youth Department in Eastern Virginia and traveled to the hamlet of Franklin Springs, Georgia, to take up a new academic career.

I returned to Virginia in 1960, married Carol Lee, organized the Banton Street Pentecostal Holiness Church in Richmond and later pastored the Arlington Pentecostal Holiness Church in Falls Church, Virginia. After the birth of our first child, Mary Carol, I returned to Emmanuel College in 1962. Our family lived in Georgia for the next thirteen years, teaching and planting a new church in nearby Hartwell, Georgia. In the midst of this busy time, I felt that I should further my graduate education at the University of Georgia, which was just thirty miles from my home. After applying for a "predoctoral assistantship," I was granted a full ride with a tax-free stipend for the next two years.[7]

At Georgia, I was assigned to the renowned history professor Dr. Horace Montgomery, the author of the classic book *Cracker Parties*. My field was Social and Intellectual History. This referred to the history of ideas, which allowed me to write on church history. For my M.A. degree, I wrote the history of Emmanuel College, which was published in 1968. I then moved on to my Ph.D. degree. Although Montgomery was a deacon in the Athens Unitarian/Universalist Church, he insisted that I write a history of the Pentecostal movement in America. As usual, I was somewhat of a curiosity in my classes and among my fellow students, being the first Pentecostal most of them had ever seen—especially in graduate school. Although I was pastoring a new church and building a new sanctuary, I pursued my studies with passion.

I'll never forget my final interview with the dean of the history department, Dr. Joseph Parks. He implored me to leave the Pentecostal movement and "make something of yourself." After thanking him for my wonderful time at the university, I politely declined his advice. I have been eternally grateful that I didn't abandon my heritage at this point. My 1967 dissertation, titled "The Pentecostal Movement in the United States," was published in 1971 as *The Holiness Pentecostal Movement in the United States* by Eerdmans, a Calvinist press in Grand Rapids, Michigan. To my surprise, this book made waves in the academic world, being reviewed in many scholarly and popular journals. In fact, this book opened many future doors for me in both academia and the broader Church world.

The Jesus Movement

In the midst of these early academic and pastoral years, I became aware of a new phenomenon in California known as the "Jesus Movement." I'd heard Dave Wilkerson speak about his ministry to drug addicts in New York City and had read his book *The Cross and the Switchblade*. In fact, he had recruited Emmanuel College students to help him in the very first days of his Teen Challenge ministry. Later, at the World Pentecostal Conference in Dallas, Texas, in 1970 I heard Wilkerson tell the story of what he called the "Jesus Persons" who were turning to Jesus Christ en masse in all parts of the nation. At this same conference, I had the privilege of addressing the crowd of ten thousand people. We'd heard of the horrible spread of the drug culture and the devastation that was being wreaked on a whole generation of young people who we called "hippies," "potheads" and "speed freaks." We worried that an entire generation of young people was headed straight to hell. Now suddenly, we saw a ray of hope for the future. Wilkerson spoke openly of the "thirty-second cure" for drug addiction, referring to the "baptism in the Holy Spirit." The successful cure rate for these former drug addicts who became Pentecostal believers was 80 percent, compared with the 2 percent rate in federal drug programs.

I was excited to read about the Jesus Movement in California under the leadership of Chuck Smith. What struck me was an incredible story in *Time* magazine in 1971 that told of Christian coffee houses and street meetings where thousands of hippies were being converted and delivered from drugs. Most astounding was the photo of a bearded young Catholic man carrying a heavy cross, with the caption "A young Catholic speaks in tongues." Somehow, I sensed that the idea of Catholics speaking in tongues would pose huge theological issues in the future.[8]

What I heard about Smith was equally incredible. Smith was the pastor of the small Calvary Chapel Foursquare Pentecostal Church in Costa Mesa, California. During a Sunday night service, about a dozen hippies showed up unexpectedly. They were dirty, shirtless, loud and smelled of alcohol and drugs. An older member of the church sent a note to Smith that read, "When are you going to throw them out?" Smith's reply was, "I'm not going to throw them out. They were created in the image of God."

The next Sunday night, the church overflowed with hippies who sat on the floor and even on the platform. Some of the older saints stalked out of the church—never to return—after some of the hippies sat in "their seats." Amazingly, Smith chose the smelly hippies over the critics and a revolution began that turned Southern California upside down. In the next two years, Chuck Smith baptized more than fifteen thousand former drug addicts in the waters of the Pacific Ocean. News of the California revival spread across the nation as thousands of hippies flooded into local churches everywhere.

My Own Jesus Movement

I shared the news of the Jesus Movement with my small congregation of about a hundred people in Hartwell, and we all prayed that we could share in what we saw as a movement of God.

Every Sunday night as I drove through town to preach in my church, I passed a large shopping mall parking lot where hundreds of teenagers gathered on weekend nights. Residents of the community were concerned about drugs and sex going on there in the dark of the night. I often wondered how we could reach these young people who would probably never enter my church. The answer came from an elderly woman in the church, Dollie Stovall, who reprimanded me for not doing something to reach them. So I asked some Emmanuel College students to go with me to the mall and to make plans for future witnessing. After an awesome time of prayer in the church, we went to the parking lot "just to look around" and "to case the joint."

Suddenly, one of the girls began to weep, saying that we had to do something "tonight." Reluctantly, I took my guitar out of the trunk and we began to sing "Michael, Row the Boat Ashore." I felt this song wouldn't offend anyone. Before long, cars began to fill the lot and kids began to get out of their cars and gathered around us in a circle. We sang any song they requested, including "Amazing Grace" and "What a Friend We Have in Jesus." Suddenly, a young teenage boy fell on the pavement by my car and began to cry out for mercy. After I led him to the Lord, he stood and gave one of the most eloquent and impassioned altar calls I'd ever seen. In the months that followed, several teens were converted as we went to the parking lot every weekend, even throughout the cold winter months.

Soon the pastors of the local Baptist, Methodist and Church of God congregations came to see me and told of a great revival breaking out among their youth members with all-night prayer meetings and lock-ins in the churches. In a short time, many of the churches in town joined with me to rent an old abandoned theater on the city square. There, hundreds of teenagers from all local churches gathered on Sunday nights for worship and praise. It was a marvelous time for our church and for the city. In fact, the first young man who was converted on the first night on the parking lot preached the Gospel from my pulpit a few months later.

The Pentecostal Methodists of Chile

In 1966, in the midst of all this activity, I was invited to visit Chile with a team from Oral Roberts University. Our group was led by Dr. R. O. Corvin, provost of Oral Roberts University and an old friend of the family. The Chilean Pentecostals had sent a delegation to Tulsa to ask Oral Roberts to help build a Pentecostal University in Chile. While in Tulsa doing research on my Ph.D. dissertation, I met the group, which included Javier Vasquez, pastor of the Jotabeche Pentecostal Methodist Church in Santiago. With forty thousand members, this church was at the time the largest

Protestant church in the world. Although my Spanish was very weak, I was invited to go along as an "interpreter." This was the beginning of many trips to Chile, which eventually led to helping create an affiliation between the Pentecostal Holiness Church in the United States and the Pentecostal Methodist Church of Chile.

One of the major outcomes of the Chilean venture was the arrival of five Chilean students, who came in 1967 to enroll in Emmanuel College. I assumed that they had money for tuition, but quickly discovered that they were expecting the Pentecostal Holiness Church to pay all their costs. When my wife and I met them at the Atlanta airport, I immediately realized that I would be their American "daddy." In addition, I would have to serve as their interpreter, raise their financial support and find homes where they could live. It was a monumental task. Their names were Eduardo Duran, his wife Raquel Duran, Alexia Fredes, Gamalier Mora and Eugenio Ramirez. Through the generosity of Emmanuel College and friends from Tulsa, Oklahoma, and Greenville, South Carolina, we were able to pilot them through Emmanuel College. Later on, Pastor Vasquez's son Jorge and his wife, Isabella, and others enrolled in Holmes College of the Bible in Greenville, South Carolina.[9]

For two years, the first five Chilean students attended my church in Hartwell and before long were singing in the choir and playing instruments in the orchestra. Taking care of the students helped to cement the relationships between the Pentecostal Holiness churches in Chile and in the United States. In 1993, upon the death of Javier Vasquez, Duran succeeded him as pastor of the Jotabeche congregation which by then had some three hundred thousand members and adherents. In the years that followed, I visited Chile more than twenty times.

The Society for Pentecostal Studies

Although I was busy and happy in my pastoral and teaching ministries, I also wanted to get my dissertation published. I first went to the publishing house of the Pentecostal Holiness Church, but they told me that the book would never sell enough copies to justify the investment. Next I sent it to the University of Georgia Press for them to evaluate. After a long time, I was told to meet with Ed Harrell, who had been a reader for the press. Harrell lectured me for not doing complete "runs" of the major Pentecostal periodicals. Although I'd read hundreds of pages in the major magazines, I couldn't say that I'd seen every single page. Harrell said that if I did this additional research and incorporated it into the manuscript, I'd have a good book. So I determined to do just that.[10]

As a result, in the summer of 1968, I took a long research trip to various Pentecostal headquarters to read their periodicals. When I arrived in Cleveland, Tennessee, I read all the copies of the *Church of God Evangel*. While there, I met with Charles Conn, the great historian of the church. They freely opened all their archives to me, and I found it especially helpful to read the journals of A. J. Tomlinson. While in Cleveland, I also met Dr. Horace Ward, who was serving as the dean of students at Lee College. We became fast friends and carried on endless discussions about Pentecostal history and theology. At his invitation, I went back to Lee twice to speak in chapel to the whole student body. Horace and I felt the exhilaration and joy of discovering kindred Pentecostal spirits. We soon began to discuss the possibility of calling a group of Pentecostal scholars together in a colloquium in the near future.

On my trip to Springfield, Missouri, I visited the Assemblies of God archives where I did a research run of the

Pentecostal Evangel. Again, I was treated like royalty and given access to the inner sanctum of the archives. The first person I met on this trip was the great historian William Menzies. He'd already read the microfilm version of my dissertation and was eager to discuss the history of the Pentecostal movement. According to my church teachings, the Assemblies of God people weren't considered "sanctified" and were therefore less perfect than us. But I found Menzies to be as sanctified as any person I'd ever met. He made a tremendous impression on me. As with Horace Ward, we discussed how wonderful it would be to organize a gathering of Pentecostal scholars from various colleges to discuss common scholarly concerns. I told Menzies about my discussions with Ward, and we agreed on the spot to start making plans for a gathering at the Pentecostal World Conference, which was due to convene in Dallas, Texas, in 1970. I promised that I'd take the lead in planning and calling such a meeting. As a result, Ward, Menzies and I became an ad hoc committee to plan a meeting of Pentecostal scholars to meet in Dallas in 1970.

On my return home from Springfield, I wrote to the chairman of the conference in Dallas, David Yonggi Cho, to request a slot on the program. We planned to hold a banquet to organize this new Pentecostal scholarly society. He agreed enthusiastically. In the meantime, I communicated regularly with Ward and Menzies about plans for the meeting. To prepare for the organizational meeting, I wrote a draft constitution based on the existing constitutions of the Wesleyan Theological Society (WTS) and the Evangelical Theological Society (ETS). The name I suggested was tentatively accepted: "The Society of Pentecostal Scholars."

When we gathered in Dallas, we didn't know if enough people would attend to pay for the hall we rented. To our happy surprise, 146 people registered and the money collected did just barely pay the bill. Before we entered the room for the banquet, I heard a disparaging remark made by a bishop, insinuating that because he wasn't a scholar that he wasn't welcome. A friend from Emmanuel College, Dr. Garnet Pike, counseled us to change the name and add the word *studies*. I immediately called an emergency meeting of the leaders and suggested that we change the name to the "Society for Pentecostal *Studies*" (SPS), which we did on the spot.

Among those who attended were the top executives of Pentecostalism around the world, including Thomas Zimmerman, David Yonggi Cho, David du Plessis and others. To my surprise, Father Kilian McDonnell, a Roman Catholic scholar, attended and spoke to the assembled crowd. He was one of the first charter members of the Society. This might have been the first time a Catholic had ever addressed a function of the World Pentecostal Conference. The main speaker for the organizational session was Dr. Klaud Kendrick, a well-known Assemblies of God historian. In the organizational part of the session, William Menzies (Assemblies of God) was elected as the first president, Hollis Gause (Church of God) as vice president, and I was elected to serve as the first general secretary. At this meeting, I also met the great Pentecostal scholar Russell Spittler of the Southern California College of the Assemblies of God. Like other scholars I'd met, he seemed lonely and unsure of his place in the educational scheme of his denomination. He immediately saw the possibilities in the new society, and later played an important role in its growth and development.

Because of my involvement in the denominational world and with the world of academia, my future years would be divided between church affairs and the educational world. It was like a tug of war where I often felt pulled in two directions. In the end, when it came to research and writing history, I tried to be a true son of the church without compromising my integrity. It wouldn't be an easy task, but I was willing to try my very best.

3

Protestant Neo-Pentecostals

In the summer of 1960, I became aware of an "outbreak" of Pentecostalism in California led by an Episcopal priest, Father Dennis Bennett, who was pastor of the upscale Episcopal Parish of St. Marks in Van Nuys, California. In its July 4, 1960, issue *Newsweek* magazine told the story of a new outbreak of tongues. I was utterly astounded to read of the events that took place in 1959 when Bennett told his congregation about his experience.

Bennett was forced to resign his parish in Van Nuys, but a sympathetic bishop in Seattle, Washington, invited him to come and lead the inner city St. Luke's Parish, which was scheduled to be closed soon anyway. He gave Bennett full freedom to worship Pentecostal style and to promote the baptism in the Holy Spirit in his church. Soon, the church mushroomed in attendance and became the strongest Episcopal parish in the northwestern United States.

As word spread about the events in Seattle, Bennett became a *cause celebre* in the Protestant world. In time, hundreds of

Catholics and Protestants flocked to his church to receive the Pentecostal experience with tongues, which Bennett explained was "part of the package." The religious press began to call Bennett and his followers "Neo-Pentecostals," because rather than join an established Pentecostal denomination, they were adamant about staying in their churches to spread the movement from within.

Although I couldn't fully understand what was happening, I took in all of this with awe. And I hoped someday to meet Bennett and others who followed his lead.[1]

I Meet "Neo-Pentecostals"

My first time to meet a Neo-Pentecostal was in 1960 when Presbyterian pastor Dr. Jim Brown spoke in the chapel at Emmanuel College. He was a highly educated graduate of Princeton University and had a professorial appearance. As pastor of the Upper Octorara Presbyterian Church near Philadelphia, Pennsylvania, he was leading Pentecostal worship on Saturday nights while playing a tambourine. On Sunday mornings, he conducted traditional Presbyterian services for those who didn't understand what was going on in the Saturday night services. Brown's church quickly became the East Coast counterpart of Bennett's church in Seattle. Hundreds of Baptists, Methodists, Episcopalians, Presbyterians and even Catholics flocked to Brown's church to receive the coveted Pentecostal experience. In my conversation with him, Brown convinced me that he was both a proper Presbyterian and an all-out Pentecostal.

In 1963, news came of a Pentecostal outbreak at Yale University. Chaplain William Sloan called the students who spoke in tongues "glossoyalies." That this "behavior" was being tolerated at an elite school such as Yale seemed beyond the realm of possibility to me at the time. All of the rejection from mainline churches that I'd personally experienced and what I'd learned about the history of actual persecution against Pentecostals made me wary. Probably the most puzzling thing to me was the theological problems posed by these people who spoke in tongues outside of our circles. As one wag said, Pentecostals had "hardening of the categories." We were unsure of anyone who claimed the exalted Pentecostal experience if they didn't seek for it and receive it the way we did. In spite of my questions, I was extremely intrigued by what I read and heard about these "new" Pentecostals.

In 1970, I experienced this new wave in a most unexpected way. In the town of Hartwell, Georgia, where I pastored the church I had planted, I made a dear friend by the name of Carol Eure. He was the manager of the local Belks department store and a deacon in the local Presbyterian church. We became fast friends by playing our guitars and singing hymns and country music.

One day, out of the blue Carol asked me, "Vinson, have you ever heard of speaking in tongues?"

I replied, "Of course. That's part of what we do in my church."

Then he said, "Have you ever spoken in tongues?"

"Of course," I said.

Then he invited me to attend a meeting of the Full Gospel Business Men's Fellowship International in Charlotte, North Carolina, at a downtown hotel. It was my first experience of charismatic worship outside of a Pentecostal church. What surprised me was that these Baptists and Methodists were truly Pentecostals. They raised their hands, they spoke in tongues and prophesied and above all, they sang our songs "without our permission."

One situation at this meeting greatly affected my life. Dr. Howard Irving of Oral Roberts University asked me to come into a side room to pray for a Lutheran pastor who was seeking baptism in the Holy Spirit, with the expectation of speaking in tongues. Four of us went into the room to pray. I had many objections running through my mind: "Has he been saved? Has he been sanctified? Does he still have sinful habits that need to be broken?" And here we were in a hotel meeting room. But aren't such sacred experiences reserved for church sanctuaries? Then we laid hands on him and began to pray. The prayers were very soft and Irving began to pray in tongues. I wondered if he was turning tongues on like a faucet or if it was genuine. At any rate, I began to feel sorry for the pastor. A short man, he wore his clerical collar on backwards, and the noise level was too low. Then Irving told him to sit down in a chair, which he called "the hot seat." In my mind, I objected because I'd never seen anyone filled with the Spirit while sitting down. Irving then reminded us that on the Day of Pentecost, the tongues of fire descended on them "where they were sitting." Objection overruled!

I then began to pray that the poor soul wouldn't be disappointed, because I was sure that he wouldn't "pray through" Pentecostal style. The volume was too low. However, the pastor suddenly burst out in a river of tongues that gushed forth like a fire hydrant! I was shocked beyond belief. His diction was very clear and as he spoke I began to see visions of sand dunes and camels. The language seemed to sound Middle Eastern. We all began to weep at this marvelous display of glossolalia. When he finished, he told us that the Lord revealed that he was speaking an Arabic-like language and that he was being called to minister in the Middle East. From that point on, I could never doubt that a Protestant could be filled with the same Holy Spirit that we Pentecostals had enjoyed for so many years. This was indeed a turning point in my life.

When I returned to my church in Hartwell, I was bubbling over with enthusiasm for what I'd seen. The church people were excited with me and a hunger grew for more of the flock to receive the Pentecostal experience. In a few weeks, we held a previously scheduled revival and many people were converted. We also saw many seekers at the altars waiting earnestly for the baptism in the Holy Spirit. We were becoming a Pentecostal church all over again.

Melodyland

Another personal glimpse of the growing Neo-Pentecostal movement occurred at Melodyland Christian Center, where I was invited to speak in 1974. Ralph Wilkerson was pastor of this huge church, which was originally built as part of the Disneyland entertainment complex. The building, which seated 3,600, was just across the street from Disneyland. Wilkerson had built a following of more than 10,000 members largely from people who had attended the Kathryn Kuhlman crusades in the Shrine Auditorium in nearby Los Angeles. In 1973, Wilkerson founded the Melodyland School of Theology with J. Rodman Williams as president. By this time, I had received my Ph.D. degree from the University of Georgia, and I was invited to serve on the board of trustees for this new school.[2]

Wilkerson had also begun to sponsor an annual charismatic "clinic" with invited speakers from all the Neo-Pentecostal movements as well as prominent denominational Pentecostal and Independent Pentecostal movements. Melodyland became an important charismatic center for several years. As an invited speaker on many occasions, I met many important Protestant, Orthodox and Catholic leaders at Melodyland.

On my first trip as speaker, I was overwhelmed by the enthusiasm of the crowds that jammed the auditorium. When I spoke, I was well received, especially in the ministry sessions following my sermons. The first time I prayed for healing and the baptism in the Holy Spirit, hundreds came forward. As usual, I called out their names as I prayed. This was normal because their name cards were clearly visible. However, the news quickly spread that I had words of knowledge and supernaturally knew everyone's name. I was shocked because I had no intention of leaving this impression. One feature of the Melodyland services was that most people were "slain in the Spirit" when they were touched. When I spoke, I saw hundreds of people fall, even though I made no attempt to push them.

Among the many major Protestant charismatic leaders I met at Melodyland were Dennis Bennett, Brick Bradford, Larry Christenson, Rod Williams, Eusebius Stephanau and others. I became especially close to Rod Williams and his wife Jo Williams. She served as the registrar for the School of Theology. It was a joy to teach occasional classes at Melodyland and to see the school grow into a major center for training hundreds of charismatic leaders. I was saddened to hear that the school eventually closed due to divisions between faculty and administrators and severe financial difficulties. But for its time, Melodyland School of Theology was a bold attempt to serve the growing charismatic movement in the churches.

The Charismatic Circuit

After speaking at Melodyland, I received many invitations to speak at various stops in the charismatic speakers' circuit. These included speaking at Full Gospel Business Men's Fellowship International chapters, renewed Protestant churches,

Pentecostal churches and conferences, and various Protestant renewal conferences. Among these were invitations to the Methodist Aldersgate Conference led by Ross Whetstone, the Lutheran Charismatic Conference in St. Paul, Minnesota, led by Larry Christenson and the Baptist Renewal Conference in Green Lake, Wisconsin, led by Gary Clark. I witnessed many unbelievable Pentecostal manifestations in some of the mainline churches where I ministered. Once in Percy Burn's Presbyterian church in Charlotte, North Carolina, I saw the entire congregation dancing before the Lord in a Sunday morning service. In the same city, I saw tongues and interpretations in the Resurrection Lutheran Church led by Herb Mirley. I also saw many of these same manifestations in Episcopal churches, Baptist churches and Methodist churches.

The church I spoke in most often during this time was St. Charles Borromeo Roman Catholic Church in Oklahoma City, near where I lived. While charismatic renewal was taking place in mainline Protestant churches, it was also taking place in Catholic churches (which I'll address in the next chapter). The charismatic priest at St. Charles Borromeo, Father Dale Dirkschneider, repeatedly asked me to speak at the monthly "Day of Renewal," which attracted hundreds of Catholics from central Oklahoma. These were indeed powerful meetings. I was occasionally asked to deliver the homilies in the charismatic masses conducted by Father Sam Levin.

One of the most exciting churches I visited during this time was the Beverly Hills Baptist Church in Dallas, Texas, which was led by Pastor Howard Conatser. After a surprising charismatic renewal in his modestly sized local church, the crowds grew so enormous that he was forced to rent the Bronco-Bowl auditorium to hold Sunday services. The Sunday I was there in 1978, more than three thousand people jammed the building. The service was very Pentecostal in my eyes and gave me hope that all the Protestant churches could be renewed by the Holy Spirit. In the light of the anti-Pentecostal stance of the Southern Baptist Convention, Conatser's church was a sign and wonder.

One of my most unforgettable invitations during this time was speaking at the Atlanta chapter of the Full Gospel Business Men's Fellowship International. I was invited by Linwood Maddox, a lawyer who headed the Atlanta chapter. To my surprise, more than one thousand people were seated at dinner tables at the meeting. It seemed like an immense ocean of people from the platform. I gave my personal testimony, which the crowd received with thunderous applause. At the end, I prayed for hundreds of people to receive the baptism in the Holy Spirit. Shockingly, many of those attending were Roman Catholics.

Later, in 1981 I was invited to speak in Atlanta in the famous St. Phillips Cathedral, the largest Episcopal church in the United States. The dean of the cathedral, Father David Collins, was in charge. He was then serving as the president of the House of Deputies for the Episcopal church. Some seven hundred people attended the weeknight prayer meeting. Here something unusual happened that I never forgot. The priest in charge of the service was slain in the Spirit and was still on the floor out in the Spirit when the lights were turned out and the church closed for the night. Out of this meeting came a very close and long-lasting friendship with Dean Collins and his wife, Ginny.

Another major stop on the charismatic circuit was the charismatic conference held each year in Pittsburgh hosted by Russ Bixler, a Brethren charismatic who had an influential television ministry in Pittsburgh. Each year about five thousand people gathered on the campus of Duquesne University. I spoke at two of these conferences in 1986 and 1987 to enthusiastic audiences. In these meetings I was a major speaker alongside such luminaries as Derek Prince and Dennis Bennett. I was aware that the Catholic charismatic movement had started on the campus of Duquesne in 1967, so to me, this was holy ground.

One night, I heard Dennis Bennett speak. Many consider him to be the founding father of the charismatic movement. He was a delight—very urbane and articulate. After his message, he invited all who wished to be baptized in the Holy Spirit and speak in tongues to meet in a corner of the large auditorium. I decided to attend and see how a mainline Protestant led people into the Pentecostal experience. I was curious to see if he followed the Azusa Street formula of three blessings—salvation, sanctification and baptism in the Holy Spirit. He said to the 120 people assembled (I counted them), "I will pray three prayers for you. The first is for salvation in case any of you are not saved. The second prayer is for deliverance from addictions or besetting sins that have you bound. The third is for the baptism in the Holy Spirit with speaking in tongues." This followed the classical Pentecostal formula that I'd known for generations. After the third prayer, the entire group began to murmur in tongues. For me, it happened a little fast and without prolonged "tarrying." But I couldn't argue with Bennett's methods. Later, this story helped me explain Neo-Pentecostalism to my friends in Pentecostal churches.

Until 1972, all my experiences had been with Protestants, both Pentecostal and charismatic. I could see and proclaim that the charismatic movement among mainline Protestants was a genuine move of God. I would soon learn that the movement was growing even more rapidly in the Roman Catholic Church. My biggest surprises and challenges were just ahead as I encountered Catholic Pentecostalism for the first time.

4

Catholic Charismatics

I'll never forget one morning in 1972, when I went to the tiny post office in Franklin Springs, Georgia, to check my mail. In the stack was a letter from St. Johns University in Collegeville, Minnesota, from Father Kilian McDonnell. He was inviting me to speak at the third annual Catholic Charismatic Conference, which would convene on the campus of Notre Dame University in June 1972. I'd met McDonnell at the Pentecostal World Conference in 1970, and he was now a member of the SPS. I soon learned that he was widely known among both Catholics and Protestants. My task was to respond to a paper McDonnell had written proposing a new theology for Catholic "Neo-Pentecostals," as they were called. I was to respond to the paper along with Dr. Arnold Bittlinger, a Lutheran charismatic from Germany.

It was daunting to think of speaking at Notre Dame, the intellectual and football capital of American Catholicism. When I was growing up, regardless of who Notre Dame played, we always rooted against the football team simply because they were Catholics. As a teenager, I'd become quite anti-Catholic after reading John Blanchard's *American Freedom and Catholic Power*. Indeed, I was probably more afraid of Catholics than of Communists or rattlesnakes. Although I'd written about Catholic Pentecostals, I was still unconvinced that Catholics could receive a full Pentecostal experience as we had in established Pentecostal churches. I also felt sure that the Roman Catholic Church would not tolerate the renewal and that Catholics who spoke in tongues would soon get the "left foot of fellowship" out of the church. It seemed inconceivable that the Pentecostal experience would ever be incorporated into the Catholic system.[1]

The Quiet Pentecostals

With deep foreboding, I boarded my plane to South Bend. When I arrived at the Notre Dame campus, I saw multitudes of people standing in line to register. They had expected four thousand people that summer, but more than twelve thousand came. I was informed that a small prayer meeting was being held in the basketball coliseum for early arrivals. As soon as I could, I hurried to my dormitory room, threw my luggage on the bed and ran across the campus to see what would happen at this prayer meeting. I'd never seen a living, breathing, tongues-speaking Catholic, and I was quite excited about the prospect. I expected that maybe a few hundred people would come early that night. But to my surprise, I was shocked to see eight thousand people already at the coliseum. In order not to be "contaminated" with Catholicism, I went to the highest level of seats as far away from the platform as I could get.

I'd read in the Full Gospel Business Men's Fellowship International *Voice* magazine that Catholics were considered the "quiet Pentecostals." So I expected a quiet and decorous meeting. But when the priest on the platform called on everyone to "stand and praise the Lord," I was overwhelmed at the sheer volume of praise that filled the place. Everyone had their hands raised, and many around me were speaking in tongues. This cacophony of praise soon turned into a beautiful four-part harmony that rose to a loud crescendo. A huge harmonious chord filled the place.

As I looked at the priests, nuns, young backpackers and older Catholics around me, I realized that they were singing in tongues. I, a "Classical Pentecostal," was the only one who wasn't joining in. Suddenly, I was overcome with weeping as I sensed that these people were truly baptized in the Spirit and were singing like the "heavenly choir" at Azusa Street. In fact, this was the first time I'd heard a large group sing in tongues at one time. As I wept, it soon became almost impossible to breathe. So I ran to a restroom and literally sobbed before the Lord. As I tried to recover, I heard almost audibly the words: *This is real. I'm doing a new thing in the Catholic Church and it will spread over all the earth. You'll be a part of it and contribute to this great awakening. You must tell your own people what you've seen and lead them to pray for these Catholic Pentecostals.*

When I promised the Lord that I would be obedient to this call, I realized that I would probably pay a great price among the people of my own denomination. Yet I felt assurance that the Lord would protect me and use me in a most unusual way to bless these newfound brothers and sisters in Christ. I really had no clue what this meant at the time. But I was so filled with the awesome presence of the Holy Spirit that I felt I could do anything.

Incredible Sights

During that week, I saw sights that were burned forever into my memory. All night, there were sounds of prayer and praise from prayer groups both inside the dormitories and those outside. During the day, hundreds of prayer circles assembled on the lawn as people prayed and ministered to one another.

Many reporters from the media, both secular and religious, covered the conference. Among them was Richard Mouw, a young reporter for the *Reformed Journal*. He was amazed at the shouts of "Amen," the hand clapping and the exhortations of priests proclaiming that "Jesus is Lord."

In my workshop session with Kilian McDonnell, more than 1,500 people filled the auditorium. The paper that McDonnell presented was one of the first proposed systematic theology for the Catholic charismatic movement. It was soon published under the title *Baptism in the Holy Spirit as an Ecumenical Problem*.[2] In it, McDonnell explained the idea that baptism in the Holy Spirit came at the time of initiation, with what Pentecostals called "baptism in the Holy Spirit" being an "actualization" of what had actually been received at baptism and confirmation. While this approach was difficult for me to understand, I knew it was the only one that would allow the Pentecostal movement to continue and grow within the Catholic system. After the presentation, we were questioned by the audience, which included reporters from the *New York Times* and *Time* magazine.

I remember a Trappist monk in robe and sandals asking me the following question: "Dr. Synan, Pentecostals believe that it is a sin to smoke and drink alcohol. Where do you find that in the Bible?" My answer was that when the Pentecostal churches were formed, there was total agreement that tobacco and alcohol were harmful. Further, since our bodies are "temples of the Holy Spirit" we should care for and not abuse them with such addictive substances. Suddenly, I was drowned out with loud "amens" from every corner of the room. At the end of the session, a line of hundreds of Catholics formed down the aisles and out the door waiting for me to pray that they would be delivered from alcohol and addiction to tobacco. Many were slain in the Spirit. One of the strangest things I ever saw came as I prayed for a young Catholic man who demonstrated to me that he could pray the rosary in tongues. I was flabbergasted.

I also saw incredible sights in the plenary sessions. The crowd was overwhelmingly made up of young people, many who had hitchhiked and backpacked to get to South Bend. From the platform, a young man sang a solo in tongues and then sang the interpretation. The only instrumental music for the eight thousand people gathered was a flute, a guitar and a tambourine. Some of the songs were new and exotic to me, coming from Catholic folk masses that had sprung up after Vatican II. But most impressively, they sang many songs from the Pentecostal tradition, including "Spirit of the Living God, Fall Fresh on Me" and the old camp meeting song "I Have Decided to Follow Jesus." Before I left the conference, I was interviewed by reporters from *New Covenant*, the new magazine of the renewal. I soon became a regular contributor on the magazine's pages.[3]

The leaders were so young. Most of them were in their early twenties and some were destined to play major roles in the renewal. Among those I met were Kevin and Dorothy Ranaghan, Bert Ghezzi, Steve Clark, Ralph Martin and Bruce Yocum. Most of these leaders were just finishing their graduate studies in theology at Notre Dame and had the dew of youth upon them. They were bubbling over with incredible enthusiasm for the revival that had engulfed them. I also met some of the older leaders such as Edward O'Connor, author of *The Pentecostal Movement in the Catholic Church* and Jane Massingbyrd Ford from the faculty of Notre Dame.[4] They were to have a great influence on my life in future years. At Notre Dame, I also met a wonderful friend: Bill Beatty, founder of the Alleluia Community in Augusta, Georgia. Although most of this congregation's members were Roman Catholic, it was an ecumenical community with a large number of Protestants as members, too. The congregation had purchased an old housing project and created a charismatic community where the members shared their lives and ministries. This was one of the new charismatic communities springing up around the nation. Bill later invited me to speak in a regional Catholic charismatic conference in the Augusta Civic Center. I felt that this was of such historic importance that I took a busload of Emmanuel College students with me to see what was happening. One of the other invited speakers was Bob Mumford, who turned out to be one of the most gifted communicators I'd ever heard anywhere.

In my session, I gave a short history of the Pentecostal and charismatic movements, along with a short testimony about my experiences at Notre Dame. The response to my message was electric. The Catholics were overwhelming in their warmth and hospitality. I could see the Emmanuel College students in the balcony. They were overcome by the Holy Spirit as they watched Catholics rejoicing and manifesting gifts of the Spirit. It was what we Pentecostals would call a "Hallelujah breakdown."

Revival at Home

When we returned to Franklin Springs, some of the students and I were asked to speak at the college chapel service and describe what we'd seen at the Catholic charismatic conference we'd attended. As I was speaking, the Holy Spirit suddenly fell on the student body and a torrent of praise arose in the auditorium. Students rushed to the front and confessed to sins and other failures. Many were slain in the Spirit and several were baptized in the Holy Spirit. The chapel was filled all day and into the night as students prayed for a revival on the campus. For more than a week, prayer was heard in the dormitories and on the campus quadrangle as students gathered to pray, sometimes all night. It looked very similar to what I'd seen on the Notre Dame campus. I was amazed that a revival came to a Pentecostal college as a result of a Catholic conference.

Pentecostals in Europe

Just after this incredible event, I was invited by David du Plessis to join him and several other Pentecostal leaders in the Catholic Pentecostal Dialogue, which was meeting in Rome in 1972. He and McDonnell had begun the dialogue to hold a meeting between leading Roman Catholic theologians and leading Pentecostal and Neo-Pentecostal leaders from the mainline Protestant churches. It was another chapter in an amazing year for me.[5]

As I flew into Rome, I sat by a window so I could see the historic sights of Rome that I'd taught about for years in my Western Civilization history classes. But as I looked across the aisle, I saw a Catholic nun reading a copy of *New Covenant* magazine. This issue had my name on the cover in inch-high letters teasing an article I'd written titled "Charismatic Bridges." This was too much for me! I forsook seeing Rome from the air and slid over to talk with her across the aisle. When I told her who I was, she exclaimed, "Praise God! What brings you to Rome?"

I told her about the dialogue and then I asked her the same question. "What brings you to Rome?"

She answered, "So many sisters in my convent have received the gift of tongues that I was summoned by the mother superior to come and explain what's happening."

I said, "Praise God."

Then she reached her hands across the aisle and prayed for me in tongues. At that moment, the plane touched down at DaVinci Airport. I truly had a "Pentecostal" arrival in Rome.

I was taken directly from the airport to a charismatic prayer meeting that convened that afternoon in the chapel of the Pontifical Gregorian University, where many American priests came to study. It was the intellectual and theological capital of the Roman Catholic world. When we entered the chapel, I was told that several Catholic bishops, cardinals and theologians were in attendance. This was another epiphany for me, as the crowd was singing our Pentecostal songs (without our permission), accompanied by flutes and tambourines. When they sang all the verses of "Amazing Grace" from memory, I dissolved in tears. They were so sincere and loving. There I met Father Francis Sullivan and other Catholic leaders.

The dialogue was held near the Spanish Stairs in the convent of the Picpus Sisters. Some of the Pentecostal participants were Dr. Rodman Williams, a Presbyterian from Melodyland School of Theology and John McTernan, a Pentecostal pastor in Rome. Some of the Catholic participants were Louis Bouyer, Balthasar Fischer and Heribert Muehlen. I presented a paper I'd prepared comparing the experiences of some early Pentecostals with some saints of the Roman Catholic Church. I concluded that in many ways, they were truly "soul brothers and sisters." This began a close relationship with David du Plessis that lasted until his death in 1987.

On the first night in the convent, I spent a largely sleepless night in prayer. Knowing what I did about the Reformation, and the deep issues between Catholics and Protestants, I felt a keen desire not to compromise truth in any way. Although I was now sympathetic to Catholic charismatics and appreciated their devotion and piety, I knew that vast differences still remained. I'd been helped greatly by reading Wells and Woodbridge's book *Revolution in Rome*, and I knew that huge changes were already afoot after Vatican II. But still I was on my spiritual guard. At about 3 A.M., I arose and asked the Lord to help me during the week. As I often did in times such as this, I turned to the Scriptures for an answer. I asked the question of the Lord, "What will be the end of this movement? Is it of God or not?"

At random, my eyes fell on Isaiah 55, where I read:

> For as the rain comes down, and the snow from
> heaven,
> And do not return there,
> But water the earth,
> And make it bring forth and bud,
> That it may give seed to the sower
> And bread to the eater,
> So shall My word be that goes forth from My mouth;
> It shall not return to Me void,
> But it shall accomplish what I please,
> And it shall prosper in the thing for which I sent it.
>
> For you shall go out with joy,
> And be led out with peace;
> The mountains and the hills
> Shall break forth into singing before you,
> And all the trees of the field shall clap their hands.

> Instead of the thorn there shall come up the cypress
> tree,
> And instead of the brier shall come up the myrtle
> tree;
> And it shall be to the Lord for a name,
> For an everlasting sign that shall not be cut off.
>
> Isaiah 55:10–13

After reading this passage, I slept well with the assurance that the movement would bear good fruit and that I was moving in the will of God. A highlight of the dialogue came the next day when Muehlen came to the meeting with a huge smile on his face. Usually dour, he seemed like a different person. When we gathered around to see what had happened, he admitted that he'd visited a small Italian Pentecostal church the night before and had received the baptism in the Holy Spirit.

When the dialogue ended, I'd planned to return home by way of Madrid, Spain, so I could visit the world-famous Prado Museum. But du Plessis, Williams and McTernan strongly urged me to change my plans and go with them to a charismatic leaders' conference convening in Schloss Craheimm, Germany, the next week. Led by Arnold Bittlinger and Rodman Williams, it brought together about one hundred leaders from across Europe and Great Britain. I reluctantly changed my flight to go with them, although I could be there for only one night and part of the following day.

When we arrived for the meeting, Rodman Williams was in charge. For some reason, I felt compelled to ask for the privilege of sharing my experience of prayer in the dialogue a few nights before. Williams graciously granted my request. When I told of my concerns about compromise with Catholics and how the Scripture from Isaiah 55 had helped me, I quoted the line about the briar tree and the myrtle tree, but said I didn't know why the Lord had impressed me to tell it.

At the end of the session, a Catholic priest and Anglican priest from Ireland came to me in a state of near bliss. They said that the Lord had sent me from Rome to Germany just to share that testimony and Scripture with them. The Anglican priest was Cecil Kerr from near Belfast, who was working with the Catholic priest to bring peace between Catholics and Protestants in Northern Ireland. Everything was ready to begin, except for one thing. Kerr's wife felt some of the same concerns that I'd expressed about working with Catholics. They said that her name was "Myrtle" and that the Scripture about the myrtle tree was confirmation that they should begin the project.

A Time of Upheaval

After returning home, I was invited by Russell Spittler to come to Costa Mesa and teach a modular class on Pentecostal history at the Southern California College of the Assemblies of God. My twin brother, Vernon, and his family joined with my family as we drove our pop-up campers from Georgia to California. This came during the oil embargo, and I was shocked to pay fifty cents a gallon for gas, which seemed outrageous at the time. Still, I enjoyed a marvelous two weeks teaching some of the brightest students I'd ever seen. During this trip, I visited the site of Azusa Street for the first time, as well as the house on Bonnie Brae Street where William Seymour had received the Pentecostal experience prior to opening the Azusa Street meetings.

When we drove back east from California, we went directly to Roanoke, Virginia, where the General Conference of the Pentecostal Holiness Church convened in the Civic Center. Since we had our camper, we just set up camp in the parking lot with another group of friends, including Paul Howell and his family, although this meant we had no bathrooms or phones. Because I was a delegate from Georgia, I was a full voting member of the conference. This was the first General Conference I'd attended where my father wasn't the presiding officer. This alone was a new experience for me.

In the two years prior to the conference, I'd been commissioned to write a new history of the denomination titled *The Old Time Power*. My only public duty was to introduce the book to the delegates and try to sell some in the conference bookstore. In the light of all I'd seen at Notre Dame and in Europe, I became convinced that the Pentecostals needed a renewal as much as any other church, and I felt a burden to share this and the incredible news of the Catholic renewal to the conference assembled.[6]

I struggled to think about these and other spiritual matters, because the conference was locked in a fierce debate over whether to move the church headquarters from the town of Franklin Springs, Georgia, to Oklahoma City. After a long debate where Charles Bradshaw, the mayor of Franklin Springs, spoke fiercely for his town, and Bishop Floyd Williams spoke for moving, the vote to relocate passed by a margin of one vote. Although I didn't know it at the time, this decision was also important to my future.

The denomination's leaders had allotted me five minutes in a night session to introduce my new book, which had been printed just in time for the meeting. After much prayer, I decided to give two and a half minutes to the book and the other two and a half minutes to a report on the Catholic renewal. I realized that this could end my influence and future in the denomination, as it was one of the most conservative of all the Pentecostal churches in the world. I decided that because you have to die once, you might as well go down for a good cause.

When I was introduced, I spoke enthusiastically about the book, and then launched into an impassioned report on my trip to Rome and the remarkable revival in the Catholic Church. I then said that we Pentecostals don't need to hide behind our name, because the "signs and wonders" inside the church were far more important than the church signs on the outside of the buildings. Further, I said that Pentecostals should pray for the Catholic Pentecostals because they had accepted much of what we were teaching about the baptism in the Holy Spirit. I felt that this was truly my prophetic swan song to the church.

To my astonishment, the whole multitude stood to their feet as a torrent of praise went up at the news of the Catholic renewal. Many were weeping and applauding. Instead of ending my ecclesiastical career that night, just two days later I was nominated and elected to serve as the General Secretary of the denomination. This was totally unexpected—no one had even talked to me about it. Because I was with my family on the road without access to telephones for a month prior to the conference, there was no opportunity for me to engage in any politics or even to talk about being elected to any position at all.

I realized that my life would now be truly complicated. I'd have to resign my pastorate in Hartwell, leave my teaching position at Emmanuel College and become a full-time leader in the denomination. Because the conference voted to move the denominational headquarters to Oklahoma City, I would have to uproot my family from Georgia and move to Oklahoma. Above all, I knew that many conflicts lay ahead because I was now recognized as one of the national leaders in the charismatic movement. It would be a difficult future, but I was determined to fulfill the calling that I knew God had ordained for my ministry.

5

Charismatic Concerns and Controversies

Two cities in Missouri were destined to play a major part in my life for the next decade, beginning in 1976. Glencoe is a small town near St. Louis, while Kansas City is a large metropolis on the western border of the state, across the river from Kansas.

A couple hundred miles to the southwest of St. Louis is the city of Springfield, Missouri, sometimes referred to as the Vatican city of the world's largest Pentecostal denomination, the Assemblies of God. During the 1970s, all three of these cities played prominent roles in the spiritual renewal sweeping the nation.

Two Directions

For several years, the village of Glencoe served as the gathering place for important charismatic leaders of both the mainline Protestant churches and the Roman Catholic churches. This group actually had its origins in Seattle in 1971 under the leadership of Dennis Bennett and 23 other leaders invited by Bennett to "understand what God is saying in regard to the renewal today" and to "have a more unified expression of the will and purposes of God." This group became known as the "Seattle Presbytery."

These leaders dealt with two controversial practices in their Glencoe meetings. One was the practice of rebaptizing charismatics by immersion, sometimes in swimming pools as done by Pat Boone. The rebaptizing of believers was opposed by Catholics, Episcopalians, Presbyterians and Methodists who practiced infant baptism. The other problem was the practice of mass exorcisms (also called "deliverance") as performed by Derek Prince, Don Basham and other leaders from Fort Lauderdale. This caused consternation, especially among some Pentecostals such as David du Plessis, who held that Spirit-filled believers could not be demon-possessed. In the meetings led by Bennett, these vexing practices were moderated to the extent that they were soon forgotten as major issues. The group also adopted a "code of ethics" as a guideline for relationships among charismatic leaders.

Another meeting of leaders took place in Tulsa, Oklahoma, in 1972, called and hosted by Chuck Farah and Howard Irving, both professors at Oral Roberts University. Although no records exist regarding this meeting, the major topic of conversation was the growing influence of the five teachers known as the "Fort Lauderdale Five" consisting of Bob Mumford, Charles Simpson, Derek Prince, Don Basham and Ern Baxter. Some of their teachings, while applauded by many, seemed dangerous to many leaders. Among those who raised questions about the teachings of the Fort Lauderdale Five were

David du Plessis, Pat Robertson and Demos Shakarian, who welded tremendous influence in renewal circles. The most controversial teaching, called "shepherding" and/or "discipleship," held that everyone should submit to a "shepherd" as a "covering" or authority figure.

A very gifted group of teachers, the Fort Lauderdale Five were soon in great demand in the burgeoning charismatic conferences popping up everywhere. In addition, the publication of *New Wine* magazine, edited by Don Basham, was designed to promote these teachings. *New Wine* soon became one of the most popular and influential periodicals throughout the renewal. The Fort Lauderdale teachers took vows of submission to each other and created Christian Growth Ministries to further spread their teachings.[1]

Covenant Commitments

In 1974, unknown to most charismatics, the Fort Lauderdale leaders formed an "elders group" of eight people under the leadership of Bob Mumford to deal with local problems in the Fort Lauderdale area caused by the moral failure of a prominent local leader. Later, Kevin Ranaghan, Larry Christenson and Paul De Celles were added to the group. Each of these men made "covenant commitments," agreeing to be under the spiritual direction of another member of the group. Their commitment stated:

> We promise to be reliable and accountable among ourselves, and to respect the order the Lord is establishing among us through our relationships, one to another. We agree to be present when the council meets, unless excused for a serious reason by at least one other member of the council. We agree to take concern for and care for the financial aspects of the council, and one another's personal lives.[2]

One of the first actions of the group was planning "Shepherds' Conferences." These events would bring together key leaders of the charismatic renewal for mutual support and encouragement. Everyone invited was to be a "shepherd"—that is, someone who had spiritual oversight of one or more individuals. However, word began to circulate around the country that the Fort Lauderdale group might try to form a new charismatic denomination based on the shepherding/discipleship principles being developed. Others wondered about the strong presence of Roman Catholic leadership in the group, especially when Cardinal Joseph Suenens became actively engaged. In a short time, Suenens invited the leaders to his palace in Malines to learn more about the movement. This prompted the group to also call itself the "Ecumenical Council." Because I was never personally involved with this group, all I knew was what I read in magazines and heard from other leaders, particularly Ralph Mahoney and David du Plessis. In any event, by the mid-1970s, two influential gatherings of charismatic leaders were taking place: one led by the Fort Lauderdale teachers, and the older group started by Dennis Bennett that had met annually since 1971.

Glencoe

In 1973, the leaders' meeting started by Bennett moved to the Marian Apostolic Center in the village of Glencoe near St. Louis, Missouri. For the next twenty years, this annual meeting was known simply by the name "Glencoe." It became the major annual leadership gathering for the renewal, as well as a spiritual think tank for settling controversies that arose. Glencoe became the location for this conference because the famous Catholic healing evangelist Francis McNutt was located in St. Louis, and his friends volunteered to arrange facilities and provide transportation of guests to and from the airport.

The Marian Center was a wonderful venue. Located in the country, it was quiet, remote and well run. Here, the leaders carried out fateful debates and decisions that would affect the lives of millions of charismatics and Pentecostals. When the group moved to Glencoe, the leaders were Larry Christenson, a leader in the Lutheran charismatic movement, and Kevin Ranaghan, a major leader of the Catholic charismatic movement.

For the group's first meeting in Glencoe in 1973, only leaders who had "transdenominational" ministries were invited. Participants were required to attend all sessions from beginning to end. And no outside speakers were invited as presenters. In the 1973 session, Kilian McDonnell presented the state of Catholic charismatic theology, while Dr. Rodman Williams presented mainline Protestant theological views. In the following year's meeting (1974), the Fort Lauderdale teachers presented their views on shepherding and spiritual authority.

After 1974, the Fort Lauderdale leaders became regular participants at Glencoe, often serving as speakers for the group. As they explained their insights on shepherding and discipleship, they began to see the Glencoe group as their ecclesiastical overseers. Through their influence, all of these renewal leaders agreed that no women would be invited to attend—they strongly opposed the leadership or ordination of women in the church.

In a short time, the Fort Lauderdale leaders, along with some of the other Glencoe leaders, joined in sponsoring two "Shepherds' Conferences." One, held in 1974 in Montreat, North Carolina, drew 1,700 participants. A larger conference in Kansas City in 1975 drew some 5,000 people. The Kansas

City meeting was awesome by all accounts. At one point, the people took off their shoes because the auditorium seemed like "holy ground." Hundreds of men sang hymns loudly in the streets and the lobbies of the downtown hotels.

Alarm Bells

While this was going on, other independent charismatic leaders were becoming alarmed at the prospects of the Fort Lauderdale leaders capturing the leadership of the entire charismatic movement. Their teachings on spiritual authority and their insistence that everyone submit to the spiritual covering of a shepherd caused deep concern among many.

The most disturbing action of all, however, came in 1974 when the Fort Lauderdale leaders announced the formation of a network of churches and pastors who were submitted to their leadership. The unspoken implication was that all independent and parachurch organizations should come under the authority of the new leaders. To many people, the shepherds were creating a new denomination that would formally divide the growing charismatic movement. In short order, Pat Robertson utterly rejected their teachings and decreed that none of the Fort Lauderdale teachers would ever again appear on his popular *700 Club* talk show. Around the same time, Demos Shakarian decided to forbid any of the shepherds from appearing in any Full Gospel meetings. The lines had been drawn. Although the shepherds denied that they had any plans to start a new denomination, few people believed them. The most vocal leaders of the opposition to the Fort Lauderdale group were Ralph Wilkerson, Ralph Mahoney, Robert Frost, Dennis Bennett, Pat Robertson and Demos Shakarian.

To deal with the growing crisis, an ad hoc meeting of leaders came together at the Curtis Hotel in Minneapolis in August 1975. When the meeting convened, most of the leaders of the renewal were present, including Pat Robertson, Jamie Buckingham, Harald Bredesen, Larry Christenson, Dan Malachuk and Kevin Ranaghan. All of the Fort Lauderdale teachers were also there to present their case. The meeting was full of charges and countercharges. At one point Dennis Bennett, chairman of the group, stormed out of the meeting, but by mistake stepped into a cleaning closet where he thrashed about among mops and buckets before leaving. In the end, little was accomplished to solve the explosive situation. In later years, Pat Robertson told me that what became known as "the shootout at the Curtis Hotel" was a "horrible encounter." As a result, when he founded the new School of Divinity at Regent University in 1982, he explained that after the meeting in Minneapolis, "I determined that never again would I be a 'charismatic.' From that moment on I was an evangelical."[3]

Soon after the Minneapolis meeting, I received a letter from Kevin Ranaghan inviting me to join the continuing group that had met at the Curtis Hotel. The 1976 meeting would convene in Oklahoma City. Strangely enough, I'd just moved to Oklahoma City a few months earlier, and the meeting convened in the Catholic Diocesan Pastoral Center located just two miles from my home. In this meeting, I met many leaders of the renewal for the first time. Although the five Fort Lauderdale shepherds were there, Robertson, Bennett and Shakarian were not. New leaders present included Loren Cunningham, Ralph Mahoney and me.

These meetings were also intense and sometimes inflammatory. David du Plessis led the forces against the Fort Lauderdale group. Simpson, Mumford and Prince spoke strongly in their own defense. The most heated sessions included desperate prayers and prophecies, some of which spoke of

"Beelzebub," the "Prince of Darkness" and a "wild boar that was loose in the Vineyard of the Lord." One of the most impassioned prayers was led by Loren Cunningham, founder of YWAM (Youth With a Mission). The intensity of the sessions carried over into the basketball court during breaks in the afternoon. While Francis McNutt, a tall and thin man, was a smooth shooter, Derek Prince seemed to be ignorant of the basic rules of the game. He would hold his opponents or elbow them out of the way.

Although this meeting didn't resolve the basic problems, those gathered made a sincere attempt to draft a statement of reconciliation that might defuse the situation. In the end, the leaders at the Oklahoma City meeting agreed that the Fort Lauderdale shepherds were not in "heresy," and that many "rumors" were part of the problem. On their part, the Fort Lauderdale leaders issued a statement of "concern and regret" for anything they'd done or said to cause confusion. In spite of these optimistic statements, most of us knew that the basic problems had not been resolved.

Plans for Solving Future Conflicts

In order to deal with future conflicts within the renewal, the group of leaders who gathered in Oklahoma City created a new semijudicial body known as the "Charismatic Concerns Committee." This committee would meet annually in Glencoe to resolve problems that might arise. Leaders of the group were Larry Christenson, program chairman, and Kevin Ranaghan, secretary and convener.

All the major streams of the renewal movement were now represented in the Glencoe meetings. Although attendance was by invitation only, new leaders were invited as new leaders arose while others dropped out. Over the years, Catholics were usually represented by Kevin Ranaghan and Kilian McDonnell; Lutherans by Larry Christenson and Morris Vaagenes; Methodists by Ross Whetstone and Gary Moore; Baptists by Gary Clark and Howard Irving; Mennonites by Nelson Litwiller and Roy Koch; independent Pentecostals by Winston Nunes and Maxwell Whyte; and classical Pentecostals by Karl Strader and myself. Many other leaders attended from time to time. Over the years, wonderful traditions developed at Glencoe, such as the right for everyone to raid the kitchens before bedtime at no extra cost. One of my favorites was "roots night," where everyone enjoyed the spirited singing of old camp meeting and country gospel songs. One major fruit of the meetings was the building of a high level of trust between the brothers who met together for prayer and discussion over the years. This unity of purpose and trust prepared the way for amazing visionary events that were later born in the quiet and tranquil sessions in this rural retreat outside the city of St. Louis.

In my first meeting in Glencoe, I made a short speech that later had major consequences. Ever since I'd written and published my book *Charismatic Bridges* in 1974, I had repeatedly spoken out in favor of having an ecumenical conference that would bring together all the various streams of renewal. The purpose would be to show the strength and unity of the movement to a curious world. The Catholics were having huge conferences at Notre Dame with as many as thirty thousand registrants. The Lutherans were having annual meetings in Minneapolis that attracted more than twenty thousand people each year. Other conferences attracted thousands more. During this era, people would do almost anything to get to a good conference. They'd backpack, sleep in parks, or even hitchhike to meetings all over the country.

Three Streams of Renewal

In 1974, Ralph Martin presented a talk at the Notre Dame conference on "three streams" of charismatic renewal. His presentation was later published as an article in *New Covenant* magazine titled "God is Restoring His People" in which he spoke of "three streams of renewal." The three streams consisted of the classical Pentecostals, the mainline Protestant Neo-Pentecostals and the charismatic Catholics.[4]

I found Martin's article very encouraging, and it became the basis for my suggestion for a major conference. I envisioned the format for this conference with separate denominational sessions in the mornings, common workshops open to all in the afternoons with speakers from all three streams and massive rallies at night where everyone came together in unity. Before long, the Glencoe leaders endorsed the vision after Charismatic Renewal Services (CRS)—the group that administered the huge Notre Dame conferences—volunteered to lead the venture. As Kevin Ranaghan explained, the CRS was "flush with money" and would gladly administer and legally own the conference. Immediately, a planning committee of seventeen leaders was formed to make plans with Ranaghan serving as conference chairman. The conference would be held in Kansas City in 1977.[5]

Under Ranaghan's leadership, the planning committee was a who's who of charismatic leadership representing the major segments of the movement. Representing the mainline churches were: Brick Bradford (Presbyterian), Larry Christenson (Lutheran), Robert Hawn (Episcopal), Roy Lamberth (Baptist), Nelson Litwiller (Mennonite), Ken Pagard (Baptist) and Ross Whetstone (Methodist). Representing the classical Pentecostals were: Ithiel Clemmons (Church of God in Christ), Howard P. Courtney (International Church of the Foursquare Gospel), Carleton Spencer (Elim Fellowship) and myself (Pentecostal Holiness Church). Representing the independent Pentecostals and charismatics were: Robert Frost (Oral Roberts University), Bob Mumford (Christian Growth Ministries) and David Stern (Jews for Jesus).

These men exercised what was called "pastoral oversight" for the conference; they made all policy decisions, invited and approved all the speakers, made all major budgetary decisions and planned all the spiritual aspects of the meeting. For interim decisions, a "pastoral team" representing the "three streams" of renewal consisted of Ranaghan, Christenson and me.

The other half of the conference leadership was an administrative oversight team, provided by CRS. They were based in South Bend, Indiana, and made up mostly of Catholics. The overall administrator for the conference was Dan De Celles of South Bend. The CRS people were called "servants" of the pastoral team and carried out all the myriad details of securing facilities, signing contracts and promoting the conference in the media. This team had hands-on experience because they had administered the massive Notre Dame charismatic conferences, which had attracted some thirty thousand people to the campus in 1973. They were well versed in the logistics of feeding multitudes and moving masses of people to the different venues. In the end, these two teams worked together seamlessly to produce one of the most important and exciting conferences ever held in North America.

Because this type of ecumenical conference had never been held before in the United States, no one knew how many people would attend. In order to pull off this meeting, the three renewal movements had to abandon their separate meetings and join together in Kansas City. Of course, this posed a significant risk, because the major source for each group's funding came from their own annual conference offerings.

Early on, the planning committee decided to divide any financial overages or shortfalls on a prorated ratio based on the percentages that each group was able to enroll in the conference.

Early estimates of the projected attendance ranged from 50,000 to 75,000 people. The plans for the meeting followed the basic "conference of conferences" idea I'd envisioned, with the various renewal groups meeting separately in the mornings for their regular annual meetings, a large number of workshops in the afternoons offered by speakers from the different groups that any registered participant could attend and massive meetings in Arrowhead Stadium at night where all participants would be together as one. While the morning and afternoon sessions required registration for the conference, the evening services were free to all who wanted to attend.

In one of the first sessions of the planning committee, the leaders agreed that the members would refrain from all forms of alcohol during the months of planning. They also agreed to fast and pray for the success of the conference. One of the more urgent prayers was for us to stand in unity as we planned a conference made up of the most diverse Christian groups ever brought together in America. Although great unity was manifest in the visionary and organizational stages of the planning, the specter of division soon reared its ugly head.

The first I heard of the problem was when Robert Frost called me about troubles in the nondenominational track of the conference. In the beginning, the concept of the three streams assumed that independent and nondenominational groups would be placed in the Pentecostal stream, because most of them had Pentecostal roots. I'd been given the responsibility of planning the Pentecostal track of the conference with expectations of up to eight thousand people registering as "classical Pentecostals."

However, it quickly became apparent that the three streams were in reality four streams, with the "non-denoms"—as they were often called—constituting a separate conference. It also became obvious that there was an intractable division between the shepherding group and those who opposed them. It was like attempting to mix oil and water. Frost explained that the only way those opposing the shepherding movement could be part of the conference was to have two nondenominational tracks, one run by the Fort Lauderdale group and the other encompassing all the others who were uncomfortable with the discipleship/shepherding group. The division was deep enough that the mainline leaders often jokingly spoke of these groups as the "wild west" of the renewal. In the end, the conference included two nondenominational tracks, which we called "non-denom A" (the anti–Fort Lauderdale group) and "non-denom B" (the Fort Lauderdale group).

The venues for the conference were located all over downtown Kansas City. In addition to the evening services in Arrowhead Stadium, which had seating for seventy thousand people, other large venues included the Kemper Arena and several large hotels. The famous Muehlbach Hotel served as the headquarters for the planning committee. The Catholics met in the very large Bartle Hall, because they constituted 46 percent of the 46,000 registrants. The shepherding group met in the Kemper Arena; with 12,000 registrants (30 percent), they were the second-largest group in the conference. The other nondenominational group attracted some 2,000 participants (15.5 percent). The third-largest group was the Lutherans, who attracted 5.6 percent of the participants. Other large groups were the Episcopalians (4.4 percent), Presbyterians (3 percent), Baptists (2 percent), Mennonites (1.3 percent), Pentecostals (1.3 percent), Messianic Jews (.7 percent) and United Methodists (.2 percent).

Some new charismatic groups were formed as a result of the Kansas City conference. A major one was the Methodist group, led by Ross Whetstone. In later years, this became known as the "Aldersgate" charismatic renewal group, which soon gained the official approval of the denomination. Another new group born at Kansas City was organized to serve the United Church of Christ. This group was led by Ray Thompson. In later years, Vernon Stoop led this group, and served in a crucial leadership role in the charismatic congresses that followed the Kansas City conference.

Excitement beyond Description

For me personally, the Kansas City conference was the most powerful and significant single meeting I had ever attended. There was exuberant excitement as the crowds began to gather for the first service in Arrowhead Stadium. Although we'd hoped for sixty thousand or more to come, we were still overwhelmed with the sight of almost fifty thousand people gathered in the stands. The music, led by Dick Mishler, a Roman Catholic, was incredible. The musicians and singers were a mixture from the different sponsoring bodies, with the majority coming from the Roman Catholics and the Church of God in Christ. The crowd sang new songs, as well as the great hymns of the church. The worship alternated between thunderous loud praise to massive singing in tongues. The first hymn, "All Hail the Power of Jesus' Name," brought the crowd to its feet with a roar of praise. The crowd also roared when the massive scoreboard lit up with a huge digital portrait of Jesus alternating with the words "Jesus is Lord," "Amen" and "Hallelujah."

As the planning committee walked out on the platform, we saw an ocean of faces and heard the stirring music that had begun before we entered. I was given the task of arranging three short vignettes of three minutes apiece each night so that all the sectors of the renewal could be represented. Each evening meeting would also include two speakers for twenty minutes, as well as one main speaker with the theme for the evening. I was asked to be the very first speaker on the first night. This service was designed to highlight the history of the three streams through speakers representing each one. My talk was on the "three streams" that made up the conference: the Pentecostals, the mainline Protestant Neo-Pentecostals and the Catholic charismatics. As I faced the largest crowd I'd ever stood before in my life, it was both daunting and exhilarating.

Following my talk, Pauline Parham (daughter-in-law of Charles Fox Parham) spoke of the beginnings of the classic Pentecostal movement in Topeka, Kansas, in 1901. After her talk, Patti Gallagher Mansfield told of the beginning of the Catholic movement in Pittsburgh in 1967. Then Dennis Bennett told of the Protestant beginnings among Episcopalians in 1960 in California. Brick Bradford spoke on the Presbyterian report on the charismatic movement that had recently been published. Finally, the keynote speaker for the first night was the conference chairman, Kevin Ranaghan. I remember perfectly how he spoke of the three streams becoming one united and "mighty river thundering over this Arrowhead Stadium waterfall." He was cheered loudly as he proclaimed that God had called us to be one in the Spirit and united "so that the world will believe that You have sent me."[6] This opening mass meeting was a mighty night that I'll never forget.

On the second night, speakers included Bob Hawn (Episcopal), Howard Courtney (Pentecostal), Francis McNutt (Catholic), Ralph Martin (Catholic) and Ruth Carter Stapleton (Baptist and the sister of President Jimmy Carter).

The main speaker was Larry Christenson, who challenged the multitude with another call to unity. New songs were repeated joyfully, including "Sing to the Lord a New Song" and "Our God Reigns."

The third night might have been the most unforgettable of all. The planning committee wanted to have special chairs at the front of the platform for Cardinal Suenens (Roman Catholic Primate of Malines, Belgium), Bishop J. O. Patterson (Presiding Bishop of the Church of God in Christ and an African American) and Thomas Zimmerman (General Superintendent of the American Assemblies of God). I escorted Zimmerman to the platform. Although this represented a risk for him, Zimmerman agreed to come. Seeing these three churchmen from such widely differing backgrounds sitting together in this stadium setting was a special sight.

After hearing from Bishop Nelson Litwiller (Mennonite), Maria Von Trapp (Catholic), Bishop J. O. Patterson (Pentecostal) and Cardinal Joseph Suenens (Catholic), the audience rose to its feet when the main speaker, Bob Mumford (nondenominational) declared, "I have looked at the back of the book. And guess what? Jesus wins!" The crowd erupted in a roar of approval and praise. The scoreboard blinked on and off with the words "Praise the Lord" and "Hallelujah." For the next eighteen minutes, the roar from the stadium sounded as if Jesus had won both the Super Bowl and the World Series in one night. We later heard reports that a flock of doves circled the stadium during the time of praise and then flew off when the praise ended. Some leaders said later that this night was a symbolic climax of the charismatic renewal and marked the high-water mark of the movement.

The last night of the conference was a celebration from start to finish. Speakers for the night included Catherine Marshall (Presbyterian), Archbishop Bill Burnett from Capetown, South Africa (Anglican), Mike Scanlan (Catholic) and Dr. James Forbes (Pentecostal). During the service, Larry Christenson delivered a powerful prophecy predicting a titanic struggle in South Africa over the segregationist policy of apartheid. In the vision, Christenson saw a white leader and a black leader reach across the political confusion, shake hands and bring peace through the power of the Gospel. Of course, this came to pass years later in 1994 when F. W. de Klerk and Nelson Mandela brought about the legal end of apartheid and a bloodless transfer to a multiracial democracy.[7]

Two other stunning prophecies moved the huge crowd to tears. I recall one by Ralph Martin that included the haunting phrase, "Come before Me with tears and mourning, the Body of My Son is broken. . . . Turn from the sins of your fathers and walk in the way of My Son." The other, given by Bruce Yocum, called for unity among charismatics and spoke of "a time of severe trial and testing" but with the assurance that "I am Jesus the Victor King and I have promised you victory." These utterances brought everyone in the stadium to their knees in repentance. The sound of weeping filled the stadium. The closing message by James Forbes included a comforting word from Isaiah: "See Me, saith the Lord." As the service drew to a close, the stadium broke out with spontaneous dancing before the Lord to the tune of the Jewish dance *Shalom Aleikhem*, a fitting, exciting and celebratory end to a historic conference.[8]

Accounts of the conference were carried on national television network news and in the magazine media. *Time* magazine said simply, "Every one had a charismatic time." The local Kansas newspaper summed it up with a headline proclaiming that this was "The Biggest, Cleanest, and Happiest Rally" in the history of the city. They also noted that the hotels and restaurants were unhappy because the sales of liquor almost disappeared—although the sales of ice cream tripled.

While the Kansas City conference was indeed an important and climactic milestone in the story of the charismatic movement, it was by no means the last of the major rallies that marked the movement's ongoing success. Indeed, I was to bear the burden of leading the next five major Holy Spirit congresses.

6

New Orleans

The years following the climactic Kansas City conference of 1977 represented a lull in ecumenical activities between the sectors of the charismatic renewal. While everyone basked in the glow in the aftermath of Kansas City, few leaders felt a desire to repeat the colossal efforts expended in planning and carrying out this monumental gathering. The idea of another large conference was discussed every year in the Glencoe retreats, but didn't gain much support. Kevin Ranaghan reported that although the Catholics enjoyed the conference, for example, there was little talk in Catholic circles of planning another one. Most of the leaders were doing what I'd been doing—working mainly in our own denominational contexts.

Despite a general lack of interest, a few leaders strongly called for a "Kansas City II." The leading voice calling for a follow-up conference was Bishop Nelson Litwiller, a highly respected Mennonite charismatic leader. Litwiller was a patriarchal figure whom we all dearly loved. Year after year,

Litwiller—at this point in his eighties—challenged the Glencoe group to make plans for another general conference.

I agreed with Litwiller. I believed that the Kansas City conference had put charismatic renewal on the map with the greater Church and with the general public. The conference had demonstrated the power of the movement and helped to advance the renewal in all churches, including the classical Pentecostal churches. In fact, I felt that the momentum caused by the Kansas City conference was beginning to wane and that the entire charismatic renewal needed a new shot in the arm. I also observed that contacts among the leaders of the churches were fading and sensed that we all needed to stand together publicly to make a greater impact in the world. I agreed with David du Plessis, who often said that the renewal must be "both charismatic and ecumenical."

A New Direction

I also sensed the need for another conference so that we could divert our attention away from dissension over the shepherding controversy that had dominated our annual Glencoe meetings. We needed a fresh start.

In fact, I was in this frame of mind when I made plans to attend the annual Glencoe retreat in 1984. As the time drew near to buy tickets for the trip, I debated whether I wanted to attend again. Frankly, I was so tired of the endless discussions that at one point, I decided not to go again. I reasoned that I was extremely busy with the responsibilities of leading my own denomination. I felt uncertainty about my future because I faced the possibility of ending my leadership in the Pentecostal Holiness denomination due to limitations regarding tenure of office. However, after much prayer, I decided to go to Glencoe for one final meeting.

When we gathered, we were shocked when Larry Christenson and Kevin Ranaghan announced that they were stepping down from leadership of the Charismatic Concerns Committee and that we would have to select new leadership. As I looked around the room to see which leader I could nominate to be the new chairman, all eyes suddenly turned toward me. Ranaghan announced that they all believed I should be the new chairman. Before I could nominate anyone else, I was elected unanimously. I tried to explain that I had always felt comfortable being a "token classical Pentecostal" among a group of mainline denominational leaders, and that someone else might be more appropriate to lead. However, the whole group insisted that my denominational background made no difference and that I had their full support. To say the least, I was totally shocked by this unexpected turn of events.[1]

The group then needed to select a secretary to take the place of Kevin Ranaghan. I immediately nominated Brick Bradford, head of the Presbyterian renewal. My hope was that he would agree because we both lived in Oklahoma City and had worked together for years leading local Pentecostal celebrations. The group elected Bradford, but he later declined and nominated Vernon Stoop, leader of the United Church of Christ renewal group, to serve in this position. When Stoop accepted, we gained the most faithful and meticulous keeper of records I've ever known. This began a close friendship that lasted for seventeen years and resulted in planning five major charismatic conferences.

When I addressed the group, I told them that I was really an activist and that I would like to see another major charismatic conference held in the near future. I was glad when the other leaders seemed to agree that this might be the way for us to go. At this point, we decided to pray about it and poll all the renewal groups before making a final decision.

Call for a Congress

Following the Glencoe meeting, I immediately sent out letters of inquiry to all the groups that might be interested. In January 1985, we called a meeting of the executive committee in Dallas, Texas, to consider the responses. We discovered that all of the renewal groups had some interest in another major conference, but all felt that a smaller "leaders' conference" should take place before a much larger "general conference" could be convened. The executive committee also decided to call for a "consultation" to convene where a final decision could be made.

In May 1985, a large number of leaders met in St. Louis and prayerfully discussed plans for the future. We decided that we would hold a small conference for about 10,000 leaders in 1986, and follow that with a very large meeting in 1987 with a hoped-for registration of some 75,000 people. We also decided that a new legal umbrella organization would need to be formed to own and operate the conferences, and we needed to make a decision regarding the venue of the meetings.

These questions were faced at another meeting in Chicago in August 1985. We formed a new legal entity called the North American Renewal Service Committee (NARSC). A lawyer from Charles Green's church in New Orleans wrote the charter, which was recorded in the state of Louisiana. In a later meeting, the committee chose the city of New Orleans for both conferences, which we dubbed "Congresses on the Holy Spirit and World Evangelization." The committee also decided to use a member of Charismatic Renewal Services, the group that had administered the Kansas City conference, to administer the congresses. He was David Sklorenko, a Catholic brother from South Bend, Indiana. I was destined to work very closely with David in planning several large congresses over the next few years.

In one of our first planning meetings in New Orleans, we held a meeting with local pastors and lay leaders to raise seed money for the congresses, which we knew would be very expensive. On one unforgettable night in a fine restaurant, the members of the executive committee were treated to an old-fashioned Pentecostal fund-raising session led by the local chairman, Pastor Charles Green. He wouldn't let anyone leave the room until the group reached the goal of $100,000 in pledges. It was an awesome evening. One layman gave all the money from a house he'd just sold. We met the goal.

One of our first decisions was to call the meeting a "congress" rather than a "conference." We recognized that many major denominational groups would bring their own annual conferences to this event, and at the same time would join in sponsoring the gathering. Because the New Orleans leaders' event would be a "conference of conferences," we designated it a "congress." The depth and scope of the congress was evident by the sponsoring groups and their leaders, which included the following: Kevin Ranaghan, Bill Beatty and Nancy Kellar (Roman Catholics); myself, Bishop Samuel Green and Karl Strader (classical Pentecostals); Ross Whetstone and Gary Moore (United Methodists); Chuck Irish (Episcopalians); Brick Bradford (Presbyterians); Gary Clark (Baptists); Larry Christenson and Morris Vaagenes (Lutherans); Nelson Litwiller and Doug Fike (Mennonites and Brethren); Jim Bevis (Restoration churches); Vernon Stoop (United Church of Christ); Wilbur Jackson (Wesleyan-Holiness churches); and Bob Mendelsohn (Messianic Jews). While this impressive and unique group of leaders represented many different traditions, we were held together by our common experience of being baptized in the Holy Spirit. We all recognized that we represented vast differences in theology and practice, but we felt called to act together to win the world to Christ, despite our differences.

As we continued the planning process and worked together representing many different Christian traditions, the committee decided that we needed a policy statement that expressed the basis of our unity. In December 1985, Kevin Ranaghan submitted an inspired document called a "Statement of Policy," which we all signed. After pledging to "accept each other as brothers and sisters . . . in His body the Church," we agreed to "develop mutual trust, fellowship and affection" as we "uphold each other in prayer." As to ultimate Christian unity, we agreed that "our hope is in the Lord." Beyond my full-time salary, the committee also provided me with an office near my home and a full-time secretary who happened to be my daughter, Virginia. Shortly after, Pat Robertson gave five thousand dollars in support of the congress; some of this money was used to furnish my office.

The New Orleans Leaders' Congress

With this remarkable level of unity, the planning committee completed plans for the Leaders' Congress which convened in October 1986 in a curtained-off portion of the Superdome with seating for 10,000 people. After months of planning and advertising—including many trips across the nation promoting the event in various charismatic conferences, in large churches and on Christian television—the meeting opened with more than 7,500 leaders from most of the Pentecostal churches and the various charismatic renewal movements in the mainline churches. Although we didn't reach the 10,000 mark, we were very happy to see the thousands who came.

I was extremely excited to give the opening address to the enthusiastic crowd on the first night. On the way to the podium, I told Bill Beatty that I was somewhat apprehensive about speaking to such a large and select crowd of leaders. His answer was, "Don't worry. You could read numbers from the telephone book and everyone would shout." Indeed, electricity was in the air as I opened the congress.

My message included the challenge inspired by Father Tom Forrest to win a majority of the world's population to Christ before the turn of the century in A.D. 2000. Among other things, I urged these leaders to join in a "decade of world evangelization" as we looked toward the 2000th birthday of Jesus. The goal was to present Jesus with an absolute majority of the world population by A.D. 2000. "We would like to win the whole world, but at least let's have half the world Christian by the end of the century."

At the end of the first session, Father Terry Fullam, an Episcopal charismatic priest, challenged the charismatics to "go behind the enemy's lines" to win the world for Christ. During the following mornings, various denominational groups conducted their own workshops and business sessions. The largest number of registrants were charismatic Catholics, who made up more than half the participants.

In other general sessions, the congress was treated to challenging messages by Yonggi Cho, pastor of the largest church in the world in Seoul, South Korea (with 500,000 members), as well as messages by Oral Roberts, David du Plessis, Bishop Ithiel Clemmons, John Wimber and Jane Hanson. On the final night, the audience was electrified by the challenge of Tom Forrest, who charged the leaders to live holy lives of prayer and consecration. He said, "To convert the pagan world, we must *be* the sign and wonder: We must be holy."

An unforgettable night came on Friday when we honored the pioneers who had led the Holy Spirit renewal over many years. They included Oral Roberts, the healing evangelist who had pioneered televangelism; David du Plessis, also known as "Mr. Pentecost"; Demos Shakarian, founder of the Full Gospel Business Men's Fellowship International; and Bishop Nelson Litwiller, the Mennonite missionary. I was honored to present plaques to each of these great men, but I was urged to hold tightly to the microphone so none of them could launch into a long message. I was especially careful with David du Plessis because I'd already heard him preach for two and a half hours on two different occasions.

Saturday, the last day of the congress, was a time of victory and exuberant joy for the leaders who gathered. We heard challenging messages by Linda Koontz, Oral Roberts and David Yonggi Cho. The congress ended with Bob Mendelsohn giving the Aaronic benediction in Hebrew, followed by the reading of proclamations in English, French and Spanish—the three major languages of North America—announcing the forthcoming "General Congress on the Holy Spirit and World Evangelization," which was to convene in the Superdome in July of 1987. The rejoicing continued when the final financial accounting for the Leaders' Congress revealed that we had an overage of $150,000, which would provide the seed money for the larger General Congress.

New Orleans General Congress

With the successful ending of the Leaders' Congress, we immediately jumped into the huge task of planning the General Congress scheduled for the following year. In our first steering committee meeting, we chose major committees that would carry out the gigantic meeting we envisioned. In the end, we chose a steering committee of 47 members. From this group, we also chose a smaller planning committee of seventeen leaders who met every three months. An even smaller executive committee made interim decisions as necessary. Representing the four major streams of charismatic renewal, this committee consisted of the following leaders: I served as chairman (Pentecostal), Bill Beatty was vice-chairman (Roman Catholic), Vernon Stoop was secretary (Mainline Protestant), and Jim Jackson was also a member (nondenominational charismatics). A local committee, still led by Charles Green, consisted of 28 members; and a youth committee, led by Bob Weiner, numbered thirty members.

I faced the tremendous challenge of keeping these leaders in unity, even though they came from such different denominational and theological streams. Early on we decided that we'd avoid voting as much as possible and work on the basis of a consensus of the whole group on major questions. With just a few exceptions, we accomplished this goal. The first decisions were simple: We'd continue the theme "The Holy Spirit and World Evangelization" and meet again in New Orleans. We'd also follow the same format of denominational meetings in the mornings, workshops open to all registrants in the afternoons and plenary sessions in the evenings in the Superdome. As before, all plenary session speakers and leaders would continue to represent the four streams of charismatic renewal.

To hold the masses of people who would come, we needed to use every large venue in downtown New Orleans. These included the massive Riverwalk facility and most of the large hotels in and around New Orleans. Paying for all this required a huge budget and capable administration. Again, we decided that each of the sponsoring groups would share in any profits or losses in proportion to their percentage of the total registration. Although the larger groups—especially the Catholic charismatics—felt that they faced more financial exposure than the smaller groups, they eventually agreed to the share and share alike policy.

The most delicate question of all was, who would be the main evening plenary speakers? Each stream could choose their major evening speakers with the approval of the entire steering committee. As at previous similar conferences, each evening would include three speakers, one major and two minor, who would be chosen to represent all the various people attending the congress. We made a sincere attempt to present a balance relating to gender, ethnicity and denominational identities.

Because I represented the Pentecostals, I felt strongly that we should invite German evangelist Reinhard Bonnke as an evening speaker. I'd met him in 1982 at the World Pentecostal Conference in Nairobi, Kenya, and was greatly impressed with his ministry, especially his mass healing crusades in Africa. Because the conference theme focused on the Holy Spirit and world evangelization, I felt that Bonnke was the perfect speaker, even though he wasn't well known in America at the time.

The way he was invited bordered on the miraculous. On a trip to the National Religious Broadcasters in Washington in January 1986, David Sklorenko and I set up a booth advertising the congress. One afternoon Steven B. Stevens, a friend of mine, came by the booth and offered us two free business-class tickets to visit South Africa. These were given gratis by South African Airways. At the time, South Africa was under fire from the American State Department because of the racial policy known as apartheid, and the airline was trying to curry favor with any Americans they could. When we explained that we wanted to visit Zimbabwe to invite Bonnke to the United States for the New Orleans Congress, Stevens offered to pay for this trip, also.

In April, Sklorenko and I arrived in Zimbabwe, where we visited Bonnke's crusade in the capital city of Harare. The tent, which seated 37,000 people, overflowed for the services. I saw Muslims bring their afflicted children to the crusade for prayer, and many were converted to Christ through miracles of healing. We also attended the "Fire Conference," where more than 3,000 pastors were taught by the Bonnke team, which included the Reverend Bob Schuler of Crystal Cathedral fame. When we met Bonnke, he was very happy to accept our invitation. On our return, we learned that some Roman Catholics were unhappy with Bonnke and were reluctant to approve his coming. However, after Bonnke was investigated by Tom Forrest, the Catholics approved his coming. This was his first major invitation to the United States, and ultimately it greatly increased his financial support from America. Other main evening speakers were E. V. Hill, Bob Mumford and Tom Forrest.

Parades and Other Potential Problems

The steering committee faced other major decisions, including the involvement of Full Gospel Business Men's Fellowship International (FGBMFI) and Women's Aglow, as well as the question of having a parade. Since 1977, Demos Shakarian and the FGBMFI had supported all our efforts. In fact, Jerry Jensen, editor of the FGBMFI *Voice* served on the steering committee. We decided to invite the FGBMFI to sponsor a giant banquet session. In like manner, the Women's Aglow ministry, led by Jane Hanson, another member of the steering committee, sponsored a dinner for the women.

Since New Orleans is famous for its parade tradition, especially Mardi Gras, I felt that the congress should sponsor a great parade as a public witness for Christ and the power of the Holy Spirit. When I suggested this to the steering committee, however, I stood almost alone. But I stood my ground, and over the initial objections of Jamie Buckingham, the vote was passed half-heartedly. Soon, we were inviting all those who came to be prepared for the parade with banners, floats and bands.

One problem that loomed over the Congress was the negative attitude of Jimmy Swaggart, whose church and college were only 75 miles from New Orleans. When Swaggart refused to endorse the congress, many people—including the press—wondered why. It turned out that Swaggart had just written a book titled *Catholicism and Christianity*, which attacked Catholics in general and Catholic charismatics in particular. In the midst of this gathering storm, Dr. Jerry Melilli and a large group of Pentecostal and charismatic pastors in Baton Rouge invited me to come in September and address the group. To my surprise, about a hundred pastors came to hear me and express their support for the congress in spite of Swaggart's opposition. At this point, I feared for Swaggart's future; as I told many friends at the time, it was spiritual suicide to attack a genuine move of the Holy Spirit. Sadly, my prophetic words eventually came to pass.

Another unexpected challenge concerned the developing presidential primaries for the 1988 election. As we were planning the congress, Pat Robertson announced his candidacy for the Republican nomination. When his campaign requested a booth at the congress, the planning committee was divided. Although most of the charismatics were probably conservative and Republican, there were a significant number of more liberal Democrats on the committee. Despite Robertson's gift to the congress, the committee voted not to allow any candidates to place booths inside the main arena, although they could be placed in other venues. I'd attended Robertson's announcement in Constitution Hall in Washington, D.C., and regretted that we couldn't support him, because he was obviously one of us.

In the meantime, I was consumed with the challenge of planning one of the most complex religious conferences ever assembled in the United States. In the end, we were able to put together 114 workshops and 115 booths for a congress composed of fifteen different conferences and 124 speakers. We also faced the very costly task of paying for all the venues and the travel expenses of all the speakers, as well as providing a small honorarium for each one. With the dedicated work of David Sklorenko and the staff of Charismatic Renewal Services (CRS), we were able to plan the sessions, print the brochures and the program booklet and book all the travel arrangements for the speakers and committee members. With the grace and goodwill of everyone involved, we were able to make this gigantic logistical challenge work.

During 1986 and 1987, I traveled almost constantly to stir up interest in both congresses, as well as speaking in several conferences around the world. These trips included speaking at the annual meeting of the FGBMFI, the annual conference of the Lutheran Charismatic Renewal in Minneapolis, the General Convocation of the Church of God in Christ, the Pittsburgh Charismatic Conference, the International Church of the Foursquare Gospel, the Church of God of Prophecy General Assembly, Oral Roberts's ICBM conference in Tulsa, Oklahoma and Freda Lindsay's CFNI College in Dallas. At the same time, I put in appearances on Pat Robertson's *700 Club,* Paul Crouch's *PTL* program on TBN and David Mainse's *100 Huntley Street* in Toronto. In between these engagements, I traveled to Africa two times, spoke in Singapore, visited Korea and preached for David Yonggi Cho and spoke in Hong Kong. I also planned and conducted Pentecost celebrations in Oklahoma City each year with crowds of up to five thousand people.

The Congress Arrives

After all this work, the General Congress on "The Holy Spirit and World Evangelization" finally began on the evening of July 22, 1987. As members of the steering committee entered from behind the curtains, we saw more than 35,000 excited people in the stands of the Superdome. A two-trumpet fanfare opened the congress. This was done as in ancient Israel when two trumpets announced a general meeting of all the Twelve Tribes. We felt that we now had at least twelve of the major tribes of Christianity gathered under one roof. The congress brochure reflected the theme, "Blow the Trumpet in Zion . . . Call an Assembly . . . Gather the People."

I felt honored to give the opening keynote address, calling the congress to order. The atmosphere was electric as the huge mass of charismatics and Pentecostals shouted aloud "with the voice of triumph." As Kevin Ranaghan once remarked, "When the meeting begins, you just watch as it unfolds." In my opening address, I repeated the challenge that I'd given in the Leaders' Congress a year earlier concerning a "decade of world evangelization":

> How wonderful it would be if we, the Christian community, could present to our Savior the gift that He would desire most—an absolute majority of the population of the world. To do this would require the greatest revival and outpouring of the Holy Spirit in the history of the Church. . . . We are to be fishers of men, as Jesus said. The first job is to catch the fish. They can then be cleaned and sorted out later.

Jamie Buckingham announced that this was "probably the greatest gathering of Christian leaders ever assembled in the history of the United States of America." The singing was joyous and enthusiastic. Hundreds of participants danced in the aisles as Michael Green and the music ministry led the worship. He said, "We've taken a football arena and have turned it into a tabernacle of prayer." At one point, hundreds of children sang and danced as they circled the outer aisles holding banners from many nations of the world. One observer, Thomas Nickel, said of the scene: "Thirty thousand, half Catholic; the other half denominational charismatics, Messianic Jews and old line Pentecostals, so blended together that it was impossible to determine to which category each belonged." Dennis Bennett described the scene as "a very marvelous and Spirit-filled three-ring circus in that one could not possibly keep track of everything." The crowd cheered the speakers as if they were rock stars.

The main speaker for the first night was E. V. Hill, who commented, "If you are not on fire, your wood is wet. And if your bell is not ringing, your clapper is broken." He brought the crowd to its feet as he called the congress to follow a life of holiness. Although Billy Graham had been invited to be a main speaker, he sent a videotaped message saying:

> I rejoice with you at the goals of your congress, and I thank God for the vital role your movement is having in bringing about a spiritual awakening in this century. Today it is encouraging to see the Holy Spirit moving in His church across North America and in other parts of the world toward the goal of bringing to others a saving knowledge of Jesus Christ.[2]

Each night, the excitement and enthusiasm of the first evening continued. On Thursday, Bob Mumford challenged the congress to "equip the saints" for world evangelization.

The Friday evening session was definitely unique. Reinhard Bonnke's message on "signs and wonders" concluded with an altar call for salvation. After explaining what it meant to be "saved," more than fifteen thousand people stood to answer the call to conversion. Thinking that they had misunderstood what he was saying, Bonnke repeated the call. Again, almost half of the people stood to pray the sinner's prayer. After many of these seekers went to the prayer rooms, Bonnke began to pray for the sick. The Superdome crowd was amazed as people with handicaps began to walk, a deaf man received instant healing and one woman who had been blind in one eye for forty years was suddenly able to see again.

In the review of the session afterward, the committee discussed the phenomenon of Bible-carrying registrants praising God and speaking in tongues as they went to be "saved." Kevin Ranaghan explained that they were probably Catholics who would "come to Jesus" every night, not understanding the culture of the Protestant altar call. In later years, Bonnke told me that the New Orleans meeting led to a meteoric rise in his support from the United States. Before New Orleans, most of his financial support had come from Germany. He eventually moved to Orlando, Florida.

Other plenary speakers from the forty denominations involved made dynamic contributions in the plenary sessions. They included: Dorothy Ranaghan, Kenneth Copeland, Bob Weiner, Carl Richardson, Bishop Alden Hathaway, Joanne Shetler and David Mainse.

One of my most memorable personal moments occurred when I visited the Episcopal conference where 2,400 had gathered. I was privileged to present to Dennis Bennett an award on behalf of the entire congress for his pioneering work in sparking the charismatic renewal in 1960. I told the cheering conferees that without Bennett, the congress would have never happened. He and his wife, Rita, also presented outstanding workshops at the congress.

On Saturday afternoon, the congress moved outside to watch the parade that moved down Canal Street. It turned out to be the outstanding public evangelistic event of the congress. In all, there were 25 blocks of marchers, with singers and bands that sang and danced down the streets. Among the many floats in the parade was one where I, along with Stoop, Beatty and Jackson, threw souvenir coins to the masses lining the streets. A headline in a New Orleans newspaper screamed, "Rosary beads fly in spirited parade." The media reported that this was the largest parade in the history of the city other than the traditional Mardi Gras parades. As the parade participants and spectators marched into the Superdome, they were serenaded by a music group from Jews for Jesus singing "When the Saints Go Marching In."

Other outstanding events of the congress were the Full Gospel Business Men's Fellowship International dinner featuring Demos Shakarian and the Women's Aglow luncheon featuring Jane Hansen. The most attended workshop was led by John Wimber. More than three thousand people saw him lead a session where there was holy laughter, falling in the Spirit and many other manifestations of the Holy Spirit's work. These signs of the Spirit prefigured the controversial "exotic manifestations" that appeared in the Toronto Vineyard a few years later.

On the final unforgettable night, Father Tom Forrest challenged the congress to "move it out" in the style of a John Wayne movie. His most memorable statement was that the only way evangelization could occur was "together." Although this idea was later challenged by Roman Catholic critics, the crowd stood to its feet and cheered the idea of Catholics and Protestants evangelizing together. Another speaker, Earnestine Reems, brought the crowd to its feet as she challenged the congress to "go into all the world and preach the Gospel to every creature."

The press gave the congress high visibility as stories sent by wire services appeared in papers across the nation. One story told of Simon Ngugi, a clergyman from Kenya with thirteen children, who sold his only milk cow to buy a ticket to New Orleans. In covering the congress, a *Christianity Today* photographer randomly took a photo of a woman worshiping in the Spirit, which appeared in the September issue. The woman happened to be Bobbie Hromas, the granddaughter of Charles Fox Parham, a founding father of world Pentecostalism. In his wildest imagination, Parham couldn't have conceived of such a congress, which proved that the experience of baptism in the Holy Spirit was now a vital part of the entire Body of Christ.[3]

The New Orleans Congress did indeed breathe new life into the charismatic movement in America and around the world. It also signaled that the years of division over the shepherding/discipleship movement were now in the past. To be sure, other issues would arise in the future, but we'd demonstrated that we could face and overcome the deepest and most serious challenges to our unity.

Perhaps the most important issue that continued to provoke discussion and criticism after New Orleans was the rising tide of prosperity teachings of several televangelists such as Kenneth Copeland, Fred Price, Joyce Meyer and Creflo Dollar. Although the prosperity issue never formally divided the movement, it continues to this day to simmer beneath the surface. In my position of leadership, I was forced to think through this issue and seek to balance the strongly held views of my friends on all sides of the question.

7

The Prosperity Gospel

For most of my life, I've been aware of a subtheme of the Pentecostal culture known as the "prosperity gospel." Although some people have never heard of it, this amazing movement among Pentecostals and charismatics has spread around the world with the force and velocity of a raging wildfire in a dry forest.

I didn't pay much attention to prosperity teachings as a young minister. I only knew that my father and most of my friends opposed it, probably because it had never been part of the Pentecostal ethos. Most of my Pentecostal friends were average working people, some who were middle class, but also many who were quite poor. The idea of "prospering" because of our faith seemed to be materialistic and, therefore, far from the pursuit of inner holiness and Pentecostal power that filled our theology and preaching.

As I matured and ministered as a pastor, college professor and national leader, I came to know many of the prosperity teachers and some became close personal friends. I was torn by what I heard from other friends who strongly opposed the prosperity gospel and what I saw and heard from friends who promoted the prosperity message. Later, after preaching in many nations, I saw the prosperity movement up close and personal, especially in Korea and Africa. I also became a close friend to such leaders as Oral Roberts, Kenneth Copeland and Reinhard Bonnke. Over the years—after studying the movement at length—I became convinced that while many of the most radical leaders espoused crass and materialistic versions of the prosperity gospel, for many of the poor masses in the two-thirds world, the positive aspects of the movement opened new avenues of hope for millions of poor Christians to rise out of poverty and live more decent lives.

The Worldwide Spread of the Movement

Generally known as the "prosperity gospel" or the "Word of Faith Movement," this movement is now an international force that is gaining millions of enthusiastic followers around the world. Led by popular teachers and evangelists such as Kenneth Copeland, David Yonggi Cho and Reinhard Bonnke, the teaching has inspired some of the largest churches and evangelistic crusades in the history of the Church.

In South Korea, the prosperity teaching is part of the attraction in David Yonggi Cho's Yoido Full Gospel Church, which has more than 800,000 members, the largest church in history. In Africa, Reinhard Bonnke weaves prosperity themes in his gigantic crusades that attract up to and over a million people in one service. In Nigeria, prosperity teaching reverberates in the preaching of David Oyedepo and in his Canaanland Church in Lagos, which seats some 55,000 people and is always full to overflowing. Prosperity is also a core teaching of

Bishop Enoch Adeboye and his Redeemed Christian Church of God, which conducts a monthly all-night prayer meeting outside of Lagos that regularly attracts some 300,000 people. Even more, every December, some five million people jam onto a larger field for a prayer meeting led by Adeboye that is one of the largest gatherings of human beings on the planet. In India, crowds of half a million have gathered to hear American healing evangelist Benny Hinn. Around the world, other preachers call for a new age of health, prosperity and wealth among Christians.

In the United States, millions tune in every day to hear Kenneth Copeland proclaim the prosperity message on his *Believer's Voice of Victory* television program, while Kenneth Hagin Jr. teaches prosperity principles in his Rhema Bible Institute in Broken Arrow, Oklahoma. In nearby Tulsa, the world-famous Oral Roberts University has proclaimed the prosperity message of its founder, Oral Roberts, whom many see as the father of the post–World War II healing and prosperity movements.

At the same time, opponents of the movement such as Hank Hanegraaff and Ole Anthony fill the airwaves and Internet blogs with lurid denunciations of the movement.[1] Also, on college and university campuses, theologians and professors from many theological backgrounds regularly and sharply criticize the movement for its unabashed materialism and conspicuously gaudy displays of airplanes, fancy cars and expensive mansions.

However, I've always had a problem with their criticism. I've wondered, "If the prosperity movement is so evil, why is it gaining such a vast following among the poor who the critics claim should be offended by the teachings of the movement?" I continued to study why this movement was so popular to the poor masses of the world.

Three Sermons on the Mount

Many Christians have wondered why the prosperity message is so popular among the impoverished masses that flock to hear it. In answer, we can imagine the idea of three different sermons preached on one of the mountainous trash heaps that lie outside many large Third World cities. On these smelly dumps, poor people fight with rats to salvage food and wasted products in order to survive the grinding poverty that seems to hopelessly trap them. Imagine that one day, three preachers come to minister to these people. One is a traditional Christian teacher, one is a social gospel teacher and the other is a Pentecostal preacher with a salvation, healing and prosperity message.

The first teacher—the traditional Christian—gives a message that has been heard for centuries. The gist of this message might be: "Because the poor will be with you always, take comfort in your faith. Poverty builds character and the Lord will comfort you. In heaven you will have many mansions, but in the meantime, we will give you as much relief and material help as possible and will try to console you." Some have called this a "pie in the sky" message.

The second teacher—who preaches a "social gospel" message—speaks next. The gist of his message is: "The reason you are poor is the unjust distribution of wealth, the greediness of the rich and their domination of the government and the power structures of society. If we can pass laws to change the situation by taking from the rich and giving to the poor, we can eventually help you. Just wait for us to pass fair laws. Or if that fails, wait for a revolution where you will eventually rule and then the wealth will be equally distributed. Have patience, and the government will eventually change your situation."

The third teacher—a Pentecostal evangelist with a prosperity message—preaches last. In essence, he says: "If you will believe the Gospel and be saved, the Lord will break the power of sin in your life and you can be filled and empowered by the Holy Spirit to speak in tongues, cast out devils and evangelize the world. You will be delivered from addictions to alcohol, tobacco, sexual promiscuity and drugs and you will be set free to become a healthy and honest member of society. Also, God will bless you materially as you work hard, live honestly and save your money. You can then invest in your own business and rise to a bright and prosperous future. On top of this, the Lord can heal your body even when the doctors cannot, or even if you can't afford a doctor."

Decide for yourself why many of the masses who listened to the last preacher run to find their way to the nearest Pentecostal church or evangelistic crusade to find salvation and deliverance. These are the multitudes that fill the Bonnke crusades and are crowding into Pentecostal and charismatic churches, large and small, around the world. It might be that these people are now poor, but they don't intend to stay poor. They believe in a Jesus who can break the bonds of sin, sickness, demonic oppression *and* poverty. The prosperity gospel is indeed a very attractive message to the poor.

Deeper Roots in History

The Bible offers both hope for the righteous and comfort for the poor. It also uniformly condemns those who exploit and mistreat the poor. For many centuries, the vast majority of Christians have lived in relative poverty.

At the same time, through the centuries, the traditional churches—both Roman Catholic and Orthodox—also amassed great wealth. Sometimes their wealth was carried on the backs of the poor. In time, the Church itself became one of the oppressors of the poor in tandem with the kings, emperors and aristocrats who systematically took from the poor with forced taxes and tithes. Eventually, the Church became rich in houses and lands. In the Middles Ages, in some nations, the Church owned huge percentages of all the landed wealth where it built cathedrals, churches, monasteries and convents. This led to the famous remark of Pope Innocent IV (who served as pope from A.D. 1243 to 1254). While admiring the wealth of the old St. Peter's in Rome, Innocent declared to the theologian Thomas Aquinas, "No longer can the church say, 'Silver and gold have I none.'" The wise theologian replied, "Yes, but neither can we say 'take up thy bed and walk.'" It seems that the Church practiced a prosperity gospel for itself, but not for the common members of the Church. Indeed, it could be said that the Church exercised an "option for the rich and powerful" rather than an "option for the poor."

One of the root causes of the Reformation in the sixteenth century was reaction to the heavy and oppressive toll of money sent to Rome to support the papacy and to build St. Peter's Cathedral. This led to the sale of indulgencies to fill the coffers of the church in Rome. When Martin Luther objected to this practice, the Reformation followed. In many parts of northern and western Europe, the Reformers plundered rich church lands to create new Protestant communities. In England, King Henry VIII enriched the Crown by closing monasteries and convents all over England and using the money for himself.

The Protestant "Gospel of Wealth" in the Gilded Age

After gaining freedom from Rome, many Protestant churches developed not only new theological systems but also new attitudes toward wealth. Beginning in Europe, and coming to America when the Pilgrim fathers settled in the new world,

Calvinists created what many have called the "Protestant ethic." It promised prosperity if an individual worked hard, was honest, obeyed the Scriptures and the laws and faithfully served the Lord. Then God's blessings would be poured out on those who lived in what they called "the city on the hill."

Many historians and economists credit this "Calvinist prosperity gospel" with the growing wealth in America, both before and after the Revolution. One proponent of this ethic was Benjamin Franklin, whose *Poor Richard's Almanac* trumpeted the virtues of thrift and hard work.

After the Civil War, a time of great prosperity blossomed in the Northern states because of the rising age of big industry, big railroads and big banks. This period from the Civil War era to 1900 is called by historians "the gilded age" of rich "robber barons" such as Cornelius Vanderbilt (railroads), John D. Rockefeller (oil), Andrew Carnegie (steel), James Duke (tobacco) and J. P. Morgan (banking). These entrepreneurs were mainly Baptists, Presbyterians, Congregationalists, Methodists and Episcopalians. In time, these enormously rich Protestant capitalists built monumental churches and hired preachers who would give a biblical rationale for their gigantic wealth. The most famous congregation was the Riverside Church in New York City, which was built with Rockefeller money. Soon preachers were tickling the ears of these rich American capitalists in sermons that soothed their consciences, while others wrote books carrying the same message. A new genre of get-rich books became wildly popular, such as the books by Horatio Alger, which told the stories of poor young people who became rich through hard work and smart business deals.

The theological world also joined in this chorus of prosperity. One of the most famous was the Reverend Russell Conwell, a Baptist pastor and founder of Temple University in Philadelphia. Conwell's famous lectures, based on his book *Acres of Diamonds*, made him a rich man. He taught that anyone could find great wealth, even in his own backyard. In time, industrialist laymen also joined in. In his 1899 book *The Gospel of Wealth*, Andrew Carnegie taught that great wealth brought great responsibility to the rich. He and others eventually became philanthropists who used much of their wealth to build libraries and endow universities. This was also the age of "social Darwinism," when some professors taught that the rich were "fit survivors" who deserved to be rich. Sadly, this teaching—done in the name of evolutionary "science"—was later used in support of white supremacy in the American South and in support of Nazism in Germany.[2]

Redemption and Lift

In the twentieth century, Donald McGavran, a missiologist and missionary to India, proposed the idea of "redemption and lift." In his 1955 book *The Bridges of God* and his 1970 book *Understanding Church Growth*, McGavran pointed out that the greatest church growth has occurred as the result of mass evangelistic movements among the poor. One of the results of these mass conversions was the lifting en masse of whole classes of previously poor people to relative prosperity as a result of becoming Christians.[3]

The reason for this economic uplift was the fact that upon conversion, former pagans abandoned their lifestyles of alcoholism, sexual promiscuity and drug addiction, becoming honest and hardworking members of society. They were "redeemed" and then "lifted" to a higher plane of prosperity because of miraculous deliverances from the powers of darkness that produce poverty.

Church history is a continuing testimony to the veracity of McGavran's theory. Repeatedly throughout history, revival breaks out among the poor and disadvantaged, sometimes producing new denominations, which then appeal to and minister to the poor. Within one or two generations, these people rise to levels of prosperity never dreamed of by their parents. The examples are too numerous to recount, but include the rise of the Baptists, Quakers, Methodists, Nazarenes and Pentecostals from extreme poverty to relative wealth in a short time.

This process is now being repeated all over the world as Pentecostals and charismatics continue to win millions of the poor whose lives are transformed by the Gospel. This, I believe, is the broadest and most positive way to view what is happening as a result of the widespread preaching of the prosperity gospel. As materialistic as the prosperity message can sound, it is also challenging huge numbers of the world's poorest people to aspire to better things. It might well be called a theology of hope.

Post–World War II Prosperity Teachings

After World War II, the American nation saw the dawning of a new prosperity built on the pent-up savings of the wartime years. The Depression years were forgotten as every level of society moved upward on the economic scale. This was true of the Pentecostals as well as everyone else. In 1948, two evangelists appeared on the scene who would dominate American religious life for decades. They were Billy Graham and Oral Roberts. When Roberts appeared on TV in 1953, he startled the nation with his salvation-healing crusades. Also, Roberts brought something new—a prosperity gospel that was attractive to many Pentecostals who had lived in abject poverty as Roberts had growing up in Oklahoma. As he said, "I tried poverty and I didn't like it."

Roberts had two sources for his prosperity teachings. One was the Bible, and the other was Napoleon Hill's 1937 bestseller *Think and Grow Rich*.[4] In the Bible, the one verse that dominated Roberts's views on healing and prosperity was 3 John 2, which says: "Beloved, I pray that you may prosper in all things and be in health, just as your soul prospers." This became the golden healing and prosperity text for Roberts and his many followers. By the time he went on television, Roberts had become the spiritual mentor of Demos Shakarian, who founded the Full Gospel Business Men's Fellowship International (FGBMFI) with Roberts's help in 1951. Soon, Pentecostals became business leaders and some grew to be very rich. Roberts and Shakarian also played large and influential roles in the appearance of the charismatic movement in mainline churches after 1960. In 1970, Roberts published his book *The Miracle of Seed Faith*, which encouraged his followers to "sow" into his ministry "out of their need" in order to reap a "seed faith miracle" harvest of financial blessings.[5]

With his headquarters in Tulsa, Oklahoma, Roberts founded Oral Roberts University in 1965, which became the epicenter of the healing-prosperity movement. His teachings also became major themes of his friends and followers. Among these were Kenneth Hagin and Kenneth Copeland, who came to national prominence in the era of the charismatic renewal movement in the mainline churches. In addition to the influence of Roberts, E. W. Kenyon's books became favorite texts of Kenneth Hagin and his new Rhema Bible Institute in nearby Broken Arrow, Oklahoma. Based on Kenyon's principle of "positive confession," Hagin built a huge following among Pentecostals and charismatics known as the Word of Faith Movement.

In South Korea, David Yonggi Cho also became a devoted friend and follower of Oral Roberts. Because both had been healed of tuberculosis in their youth, they felt a special bond. Incorporating the prosperity gospel into his Assemblies of God congregation in Seoul, South Korea, Cho built the largest church in Christian history. Later, Reinhard Bonnke, the German Pentecostal evangelist, became a close friend of Copeland and blended prosperity teachings with his salvation-healing crusades all over Africa and the world. By the year 2000, Bonnke was preaching to the largest crowds in evangelistic history, promising salvation, health and prosperity to those who flocked to his crusades.[6]

Eventually, Africa became the world epicenter for the mass proclamation of the prosperity message. Much of the growth of prosperity-oriented Pentecostalism in Nigeria and other African countries came as the result of teaching missions by teams from Hagin's Word of Faith Movement in the late 1980s. They influenced two leaders in particular who spread the message to the masses. They were Enoch Adeboye, bishop of the Redeemed Christian Church of God, and David Oyedepo, pastor of the Canaanland Church, both in Lagos, Nigeria. To further the growth of the movement, Oyedepo founded the new Covenant University outside Lagos on a campus that rivals many American Christian schools in size and magnificence.

Although some Christians in the West are offended by the seemingly crass emphasis that these leaders place on prosperity teachings, it's obvious that their followers are rising rapidly into the middle class, and in turn, they are using much of their new wealth to evangelize their people and disciple them into effective Christians.

American Prosperity Televangelists

Following the groundbreaking TV ministry of Oral Roberts, a number of influential televangelists carried the prosperity message to new heights and to a new generation. Among these were Kenneth Copeland, Fred Price, Joel Osteen, Benny Hinn, Eddie Long, Creflo Dollar, Joyce Meyer and Paula White. Some of these are African American pastors who have seen their churches explode after introducing prosperity teachings. These include such pastors as Fred Price, T. D. Jakes and Creflo Dollar. Some critics believe that the movement helps to explain and justify black upward mobility and entry into the middle class without feelings of guilt. Some have even compared the prosperity movement among blacks to that of the civil rights movement of the 1960s.

Despite their successes, prosperity evangelists have suffered over the years because of the methods of some of their more radical TV evangelists. Some of them, notably Gene Ewing and Bob Tilton, made a mockery of prosperity teachings with their strident and shameless appeals for large donations and their outrageous lifestyles. Some have accused other TV evangelists of the same extravagances. Critics have been severe in criticizing these teachers for their crass and materialistic appeals for money.

Other critics point to Scripture verses that seem to oppose prosperity teachings. These include: "Then Jesus looked around and said to His disciples, 'How hard it is for those who have riches to enter the kingdom of God!'" (Mark 10:23); and "No servant can serve two masters; for either he will hate the one and love the other, or else he will be loyal to the one and despise the other. You cannot serve God and mammon" (Luke 16:13).

A large number of academics, preachers and religious scholars also stand in opposition to extreme prosperity teachers. These opponents charge that the prosperity gospel is materialistic, takes money from the poor to support its teachers' extravagant lifestyles, paints an impossible goal of riches for millions of poor people and makes God a servant who caters to their every wish.

On the other hand, most of the televangelists continue to use 3 John 2 to undergird their teachings, as well as other verses, including: "The wealth of the sinner is stored up for the righteous" (Proverbs 13:22); "It is He who gives you power to get wealth" (Deuteronomy 8:18); "'Bring all the tithes into the storehouse, that there may be food in My house, and prove Me now in this,' says the Lord of hosts, 'If I will not open for you the windows of heaven and pour out for you such blessing that there will not be room enough to receive it'" (Malachi 3:10); and "The thief does not come except to steal, and to kill, and to destroy. I have come that they may have life, and that they may have it more abundantly" (John 10:10).

Some of the most extravagant prosperity preachers feel that donations given by their followers justify their being able to stay in fine hotels, build very nice homes, fly first class or even in ministry-owned airplanes and be paid high salaries. The usual defense is the verse, "A worker is worthy of his food" (Matthew 10:10). Many say that the apostle Paul traveled first class in his day, and if Jesus or Paul were here now, they would take jets, fly first class and preach on television in order to reach more people.

On the other side of the issue, many prosperity televangelists give generously to other ministries. Some, like Pat Robertson and his "Operation Blessing," give millions of dollars to the poor and victims of disasters around the world. Some critics think that the prosperity message offers a mirage of false hope for the masses of the poor, by saying, "If it does not wash in Bangladesh, it will not wash in America." Yet, ironically, the poor are the most attracted to the message. They may be poor, but they don't plan to stay poor. To many, the prosperity emphasis offers a ray of hope for better things through trusting God.

Despite the negative attention heaped on prosperity televangelists—in some cases, the criticism might be well deserved—the fact remains that the gospel does offer redemption and lift to aspiring masses of new Christians around the world. In the end, all religions would agree that poverty is an evil and all would call for more prosperity for the masses, even if they point to different methods of achieving it.

In my opinion, the offer of salvation, holiness, healing and Pentecostal power is still the best cure for both spiritual and material poverty. This broader message gives more "redemption and lift" to more people than all the political theories and government programs ever conceived.

8

The Third Wave

By 1980, two powerful waves of renewal were well established in the church world: the Pentecostal revival, which began in 1901, and the charismatic renewal, with beginnings in 1960. Although many important differences distinguished the two movements, both accepted the idea that a separate subsequent experience—called baptism in the Holy Spirit—occurred in believers' lives after their conversion. In addition, both movements emphasized speaking in tongues as an important accompaniment to this experience.

The most significant difference that existed between the two movements was that Pentecostals held tenaciously to the teaching that speaking in tongues was the necessary "initial evidence" of post-conversion baptism in the Holy Spirit, while the new charismatics in mainline churches saw tongues as one of the *charismata*, which might or might not come at the time of the Pentecostal experience. To charismatics, all of the other gifts of the Spirit were also signs of the infilling with the Holy Spirit.

Interestingly, the first wave of charismatic leaders stood very close to their Pentecostal brothers and sisters in their view of tongues. Dennis Bennett, while not using the term "evidence," said that tongues were "part of the package"—just as tongues are parts of a pair of shoes that can't be purchased separate from the shoes. This meant that without tongues, an individual couldn't claim to be baptized in the Holy Spirit. Rodman Williams, the Presbyterian charismatic theologian, wrote in his classic *Renewal Theology* that speaking in tongues was the "primary evidence" of the baptism in the Holy Spirit. George Montague and Kilian McDonnell, in their classic book *Christian Initiation and the Baptism in the Holy Spirit: Evidence from the First Eight Centuries*, pointed to speaking in tongues as holding a "privileged" place in the New Testament witness to the baptism in the Holy Spirit. The same could be said of many of the first wave of charismatic leaders; most would agree that while speaking in tongues was not always the necessary evidence, it was still sought as the expected consequence of the Pentecostal experience.

In time, most charismatic theologians used the term "actualization," meaning that the Holy Spirit and His gifts were received at baptism but released later. Like a timed-release medical pill that bursts into action some time after being swallowed, what charismatics called the "baptism in the Holy Spirit" was tied to initiation, although it was permissible to speak of the experience as a discrete, freestanding experience. Some critics, such as Presbyterian theologian Henry Lederly, spoke critically of actualization language as a "time bomb" theory, but most charismatics in both Protestant and Catholic traditions were comfortable with the term "actualization" or "release" rather than "evidence." Both Pentecostals and charismatics continued to accept the idea of a subsequent experience called "baptism in the Holy

Spirit," with the expectation that speaking in tongues would come at the time of the experience or shortly afterward.

As newer independent charismatic denominations formed over time, they were forced to choose between the older Pentecostal model or the newer charismatic model. The most prominent of these newer churches were Chuck Smith's Calvary Chapel movement and John Wimber's Vineyard movement. Neither adopted the "initial evidence" model of the older Pentecostal churches. In fact, Smith had been a pastor in the International Church of the Foursquare Gospel before he became the focus of the "Jesus Movement." When he started an independent church, he rejected the Pentecostal model and founded more of a straight-line evangelical church. I once visited his church in Costa Mesa when it still met under a large tent. More than three thousand young people gathered that night to hear Smith speak on Acts 2. At no point did he mention baptism in the Holy Spirit or even the existence of tongues. I left the service convinced that the Calvary Chapel movement was definitely not a Pentecostal one.

Peter Wagner and John Wimber

The other prominent denomination, the Association of Vineyard Churches, was founded in 1977 by John Wimber. In 1983, it took the name "Vineyard" from a previous church of the same name founded by Kent Gulliksen. Wimber, a former Quaker, rose to fame through his association with C. Peter Wagner, professor of mission at Fuller Theological Seminary. In 1981, Wagner and Wimber began teaching a course on "signs and wonders" at Fuller. Called MC510, this class soon ballooned into the largest class in the history of the seminary. The class became a *cause celebre* when Robert Walker ran a cover story on the class in his *Christian*

Life magazine. Readers were told about tongues, interpretation of tongues, healings and exorcisms taking place in the class. Designed as a lab class for aspiring missionaries, the class began to draw criticism from some of the other Fuller faculty members. In the meantime, Wimber's Anaheim Vineyard, the mother church of the movement, ballooned to more than five thousand members. In a short time, hundreds of pastors and independent churches from the United States and around the world began to join the Vineyard movement.

Although Wimber and his wife, Carol, spoke in tongues, they didn't ally themselves with any of the older Pentecostal denominations. Nor did they adopt the language of "initial evidence." They essentially agreed with the charismatic view of a "release" of the Spirit, which opened the way for all the gifts of the Spirit to be manifested in order to bring "signs and wonders" back to the church. Compared with Chuck Smith, John Wimber and his Vineyard movement were much closer to the Pentecostals in worship styles and in accepting the idea of a subsequent baptism in the Holy Spirit, with or without tongues.

I met Wagner and Wimber for the first time in a workshop at Emmanuel College, where I was teaching at the time. I remember Wagner as the major lecturer on the subject of church growth, while Wimber led in worship playing the piano. These two men were a super team who brought much blessing to the school and the Pentecostal Holiness denomination.

Not long after this, Wagner published his book *Look Out! The Pentecostals Are Coming*. I was impressed with the book and Wagner's grasp of how Pentecostal churches were booming around the world. Although he'd first spoken in tongues as a missionary in Bolivia, South America, he saw himself as an evangelical rather than a Pentecostal. At that time, we

Pentecostals thought that if anyone spoke in tongues they were *de facto* Pentecostals.

Through Wagner, I met Carl George, director of the Charles E. Fuller Institute for Evangelism and Church Growth. Because I was director of evangelism and church planting for our denomination, I contracted with George to conduct a survey of the history and prospects for future growth of the Pentecostal Holiness Church. Beginning in 1984, we worked together for two years. And while some church leaders were disenchanted with the study, the results were very positive. In fact, George stated that this study was one of the most successful of any he'd done for any denomination. Records show that the Pentecostal Holiness denomination more than doubled after the study, growing from 112,000 members in the United States in 1988 to 265,000 members in 2009.

During this same period, many church growth teachers began to feature teachings on the gifts of the Spirit, which they saw as essential to church growth. This especially held true in Third World countries. The whole decade of the 1980s was devoted to encouraging Christians to identify their gifts and put them to use. Many books were published on the topic, including Wagner's 1979 book *Your Spiritual Gifts Can Help Your Church Grow*.[1] Fuller even developed a spiritual gifts questionnaire that was designed to help individuals identify their own gifts of the Spirit. Special editions were created for various denominations that featured only the gifts that were acceptable in that denomination. For example, when I read the Lutheran edition, the gifts of tongues and healing were excluded because they were "not part of the Lutheran tradition." I was amazed at this because, above all others, these two gifts were responsible for the amazing growth that Pentecostals were experiencing around the world.

The Appearance of the Third Wave

By 1980, I became aware of a new view of what was happening in the church world, the idea of a "Third Wave of the Spirit" that Wagner was promoting in articles in Christian periodicals. His ideas were given formal expression in his 1983 book *On the Crest of the Wave: Becoming a World Christian.*[2] As he later explained, the third wave featured the following major points:

1. Belief that the baptism in the Holy Spirit occurs at conversion rather than a second work of grace subsequent to the new birth.
2. Expectation of multiple fillings of the Holy Spirit subsequent to the new birth, some of which may closely resemble what others call "baptism in the Holy Spirit."
3. A low-key acceptance of tongues as one of many New Testament spiritual gifts that God gives to some and not to others. Speaking in tongues is not considered the initial physical validation of a certain spiritual experience but rather a gift used by some for ministry or prayer language.
4. Ministry under the power and anointing of the Holy Spirit as the portal of entrance into the third wave, rather than a spiritual experience as is typical of the first two waves. The context of ministry is most commonly a body of believers rather than individual activities such as those of a faith healer.
5. Avoidance of divisiveness at almost any cost. Compromise in areas such as raising of hands in worship, public tongues, methods of prayer for the sick and others is cordially accepted in order to maintain harmony with those not in the third wave. Semantics become important, with terms such as "charismatic" and

> "Spirit-filled" being rejected because of their alleged implication that those who are so labeled form a sort of spiritual elite of first-class as over against second-class Christians.[3]

These points seemed to describe the views of many mainline evangelicals who desired to join the emphasis on spiritual gifts and signs and wonders ministries without the theological trappings of classical Pentecostalism. The most significant difference was the rejection of a "second blessing" baptism in the Holy Spirit with the "initial evidence" of speaking in tongues as taught by Pentecostals and slightly modified by mainline charismatics. The "third wave" was never a true separate movement, but a way of describing the way thousands of mainline evangelical churches and pastors responded to the exploding charismatic movement, which was growing inside many of their churches. To an outside observer, however, worship in "third wave" congregations looked exactly like the worship in most Pentecostal and charismatic churches. This worship included contemporary music, raised hands, prophecies and singing in the Spirit. Most important for these churches and pastors was their steadfast refusal to be labeled as Pentecostals or charismatics—although they would admit that they were somehow related to the first two waves.

After reading about the third wave, I visited several churches that fit Wagner's description. One was the Western Hills Baptist Church, a Southern Baptist congregation in Oklahoma City. This congregation was making news around town for the manifestations of the Spirit being experienced in their regular services. I decided to attend a Sunday morning service to see for myself. As I entered the church, all hands were raised in loud praise that looked like a lively Pentecostal church. Soon, the music began with worship leader Dennis Jernigan, and it was the same kind of music found in most Pentecostal churches. There were prophecies, prayers for the sick and singing in the Spirit. This congregation looked more Spirit-filled than many Pentecostal churches I knew of at the time.

I happened to sit beside a woman who was a deaconess in the church. I whispered to her, "Do you consider this a Pentecostal-type church?"

She answered, "Of course not!"

Then I followed, "Do you consider this a charismatic-type church?"

"Heavens no!" she replied. "We are Southern Baptists."

I could only assume that most of the worshipers had received a Pentecostal "second blessing" sometime in the past and were now helping renew this mainline Baptist church. As I visited other similar churches, I learned that most of them wanted to enjoy the fruits of the Pentecostal blessing without having to bear the stigma of being called Pentecostal. In many of these churches, most of the pastors had never heard of the term "third wave," but agreed that it generally described their position.

At this time, I was leading the North American Renewal Service Committee (NARSC) and editing the magazine published by the group called *AD 2000 Together*. In one issue, I published an article on the third wave by Peter Wagner as an informational service to our readers, who were almost all Pentecostals and charismatics, with the majority being charismatic Catholics. The response to the article was mild, except for a long single-spaced letter from Dennis Bennett, who expressed strong disagreement with Wagner's thesis. In this letter—which I later called his "last battle"—Bennett strongly defended the second blessing experience of baptism in the Holy Spirit with the absolute necessity of speaking in tongues as "part of the package." Later, Bennett's concerns were published in his newsletter *The Morning Watch* under the title "The Old Paths." He said:

> What I hear is, if you good people would just stop insisting there is a baptism in the Holy Spirit following salvation, and that it's important to speak in tongues, we will all get along fine. In other words, if you will drop the idea that we need the same enduement of supernatural power today that the first Christians did, with the same signs and evidences, all will be peace. . . . Peace among Christians is a precious thing but not at the price of losing the power, lest we fulfill that prophecy about having a form of Godliness but denying the power thereof (2 Tim. 3:5).[4]

Bennett believed that with third wave theology, "every pastor in town will relax and cease to seek for a full Pentecostal experience." He warned that this "would sound the death knell for the charismatic renewal." Because Bennett refused to publicly debate the issues raised by Wagner, the questions continued to fester until Bennett's death in 1991. What was clear about this debate was the fact that Bennett stood very close to classical Pentecostals in his views on the Pentecostal experience and the importance of tongues as an accompanying evidence.

The Third Wave in New Orleans

Despite the controversy over the third wave versus the first two waves, I invited C. Peter Wagner and John Wimber to lead workshops at the New Orleans Congress in 1987. Wagner's workshop was well attended and caused no problem to congress planners. The third wave idea didn't seem to be controversial at this point. Dennis Bennett also attended the congress and received a commendation from the Episcopal conference for his work as "founder" of its charismatic movement. I had the honor of presenting a plaque to Bennett.

Our experiences with Wimber overshadowed any other participant in the congress. When we first met to organize the congress, Wimber attended the session. He wasn't sure about what he was getting into at the time. He also wasn't sure that we really wanted him to come without seeing what he was doing. Therefore, he paid my way to fly to Anaheim and see his Vineyard church in action. It was an eye-opening trip. His church was very large with about three thousand in attendance. The music was energetic and Wimber led some of the songs, many of which were written by his musicians. The worship was high energy, but not as much as I expected. I saw nothing to keep him from speaking in the New Orleans Congress.[5]

However, one unforgettable incident was etched in my memory as we ate lunch at a restaurant the next day. Wimber saw a woman across the restaurant and told me that the Lord wanted him to minister to her. He invited her to our table and Wimber immediately told her that she had severe back pain. He also told her many things about her marriage and family life, even though he'd never seen her before. Then and there, he laid hands on her and prayed a healing prayer. The woman exclaimed, "I'm healed and the pain is gone!" This experience convinced me that Wimber was a true man of integrity and that his actions matched his words.

Three years after the New Orleans Congress, Wagner invited me to present the annual church growth lectures at Fuller Theological Seminary. Because I greatly admired Wagner for his many insights and great scholarship, I accepted the invitation. My assigned topic was "Evangelization and the Charismatic Movement." During one of the lectures, I chided Wagner for not admitting that he was a Pentecostal. He had steadfastly said, "Although I speak in tongues, I'm neither a Pentecostal nor a charismatic." I told the students, "If it walks like a duck and quacks like a duck, it is a duck." I was told later that in the days following the lectures, Wagner was greeted on campus by many students quacking like ducks. In 1992, these lectures were published as *The Spirit Said "Grow": The Astounding Worldwide Expansion of Pentecostal and Charismatic Churches.* The book included a foreword by Wagner. This was my contribution to the literature of the church growth movement.[6]

The Future of the Vineyard

Many years later, in 1997, I was invited to speak at the annual national pastors' conference of the Vineyard Church. This was the last conference that Wimber conducted before his death in 1998. In this meeting, Wimber was clearly attempting to guide the future of the Vineyard denomination. He was already suffering from inoperable cancer and knew that his days of leadership were limited.

In this conference, Richard Lovelace was invited to present the case for the Vineyard movement to be more of a straight-line evangelical movement, while I was invited to present the case for a more Pentecostal future for the church. More than seven thousand people were present to hear the presentations.

I was also asked to be open in sharing my perspectives on the strengths and weaknesses of the Vineyard movement over the past few years. My response was that the greatest strength of the Vineyard was John Wimber himself. As the founder, Wimber had a worldwide following and international recognition. The greatest weakness, I believed, was undue influence from outside the movement by leaders who didn't share the original vision of the founder. My message was well received.

After the message, I invited pastors who had never spoken in tongues to come forward to receive the baptism in the Holy Spirit with the expectation of speaking in tongues. About thirty came forward. The night ended with John Wimber, Todd Hunter (his designated successor) and me laying hands on these seeking pastors, many of whom spoke in tongues for the first time. A few months later, I heard of the passing of Wimber and the transition of leadership to Todd Hunter.

I sensed that this pastors' conference had been a prophetic event that clearly laid out the issues, not only for the Vineyard churches, but for the entire movement with the tag "third wave." Would the future be more mainline evangelical or more like the Pentecostals and charismatics? I felt that a great deal was hanging in the balance for a great portion of the charismatic renewal movements taking place around the world. In the end, the "third wave" was included in what David Barrett called the "neo-charismatic movement," which he listed in his 2001 *New International World Christian Encyclopedia* as having some 295 million followers around the world. Included in this number were huge indigenous movements in Africa, Asia and South America. I've questioned this category because many of the huge African and South American movements are clearly classical Pentecostal in history and doctrine and are active members of national Pentecostal associations in those nations.[7]

I feel that the final verdict still isn't in on the third wave phenomenon. It never became a formal movement. In 1991, a group of charismatic Southern Baptists—including Ras Robinson, Clark Whitten and Jack Taylor—attempted to turn *Fullness* magazine into a voice for the third wave movement. They asked me to write a lead article to start the new emphasis. I sent it in and received a galley proof. But to my surprise, the issue was never published. Thus the third wave turned out to be primarily a valid descriptive phrase identifying some newer charismatic churches and groupings, but never became an organized movement.

9

Racial Reconciliation

I was born and raised in the old South near Richmond, Virginia, the former capital of the Confederate States of America. Growing up, my heroes were Southern generals such as Robert E. Lee and Stonewall Jackson.

When I was a child, life was strictly segregated between blacks and whites. Schools were totally segregated and the two races couldn't even stay in the same hotels or eat in the same restaurants. Although we saw black people from time to time, very little personal contact existed. I remember when my brother and I played a game of pick-up football with the black kids who lived a few blocks away. We had fun and found that they were very good players. But when we told our parents about the game, we were severely reprimanded, because that just simply wasn't done. Although I couldn't understand the reasons, I did learn that we lived in two separate worlds—black and white—and that these color lines should never be crossed.

The same was true of churches. The churches white people attended were in the main part of town, while the churches black people went to were located in what was called "colored town." Most white people didn't even see these churches. Despite the color line, one mixed-race girl grew up in the Hopewell church. Her mother was white but her father was black. Despite the color line, she was accepted by everyone in the church, and as I grew up she became one of my best friends.

The Pentecostal Holiness Church was unique in town because we conducted an annual exchange of pulpits between the Black Pentecostal Apostolic Church and our congregation. One Sunday a year, the black people who attended that church came to our building and the black woman pastor preached. On another Sunday, we all went to the black church where our pastor, my uncle Lindsay, preached. I was amazed at the similarity of worship in both churches. People in the black church danced more, but the white people from our church shouted louder.

Elvis Presley's Memphis

Memphis, Tennessee, where the family of Bishop Joseph A. Synan relocated in 1951, was a bustling metropolis with a population of 482,000 souls locked in a race to beat Atlanta and Birmingham as the largest city in the South. The Pentecostal Holiness Church had decided to establish its first national headquarters in Memphis, and Dad, as head of the denomination, was required to move his family from the small town of Hopewell, Virginia.

To make money for school expenses, four of us Synan boys bagged groceries at a nearby Kroger store. We lived only one block from Central High School. Our greatest football rival was Humes High School across town, where many of our church friends were enrolled as students. One of the students at Humes was a kid by the name of Elvis Presley—a friend of some of our church buddies. In fact, Elvis, a month younger than me, lived not far from the church we attended. A few times I visited First Assembly of God on East McLemore Avenue, pastored by the energetic James Hamill, to hear the Blackwood Brothers sing, and I am sure Elvis was also present.

The most unforgettable place where our paths crossed was at the famous African-American East Trigg Baptist Church, where the center section was always reserved for whites during the eleven o'clock Sunday night broadcast, "Old Camp Meeting on the Air." During this popular broadcast, a blind boy, Lee Cunningham, would often bring the people to their feet with his rendition of "It Is No Secret What God Can Do." But we knew the service was at its peak when the stockings of the "shouting lady," who sat high up front on the platform shouting and dancing to the music, finished rolling down around her ankles.[1]

Years later I learned that one of the kids from First Assembly who came regularly to those broadcasts was Elvis Presley. Like us, he was attracted by the lively music and worship at East Trigg. In several books written years later, biographers spoke of the influence of the East Trigg Baptist Church (not the only black church Elvis attended) on the development of his singing style.[2]

Once gaining worldwide fame, Elvis bought a beautiful mansion on the outskirts of Memphis, which he named "Graceland," located on what later became Elvis Presley Boulevard. During those later years, Elvis did not attend regular church services because of the disruption it caused. But, according to Pastor Hamill of First Assembly, Elvis often slipped in quietly and sat in the front row. Years later Hamill told me that every time Elvis came, he sat weeping during the service and always put a check for a thousand dollars into the offering plate.[3]

Race in American Church History

I had no idea about the broader racial history of American churches until I went to the University of Georgia and began to study American religious history. I had a lot to learn.

During the period of slavery, from 1619 to 1865, most slaves were converted to Christianity despite the horrors of their condition and the obvious contradictions between what Christianity taught and how it was practiced. In the South, slaves were forced to join local churches under white pastors and sit in the slave balconies during worship services. They weren't allowed to have their own churches or pastors because slave owners feared uprisings. In some congregations, the slave members greatly outnumbered white members. A few slaves, like Jasper in Richmond, won their freedom because of their great preaching ability. When I was a student at the University of Richmond, a Baptist institution, we preacher students were all called "Jaspers" in honor of the preacher, whose most famous sermon was "The Sun Do Move."

After the Civil War ended in 1865, one of the first goals of many former slaves was to have their own churches and pastors. When this was widely granted, black churches—mostly Baptist and Methodist—became the centers of religious and social life, and the pastors of these churches became the natural leaders of black communities. As the churches separated racially, many black churches formed their own denominations. In 1870, the colored Methodist church separated from the white Methodists. And in 1880, the National Baptist churches separated from the white Southern Baptists. By 1929, surveys showed that 90 percent of black Christians in the United States worshiped in all-black churches. When the Holiness movement spread across the land, two major black Holiness denominations were formed: the United Holy Church in North Carolina in 1886 and the Church of God in Christ in Mississippi in 1897. And when the Pentecostal movement began in 1906 at the Azusa Street Revival in Los Angeles, it came to an American church that was already deeply divided on the basis of race.[4]

The Pentecostal movement in the early twentieth century came as an exception to the existing segregated pattern of American religious life. With thousands of white people flocking to the Azusa Street Mission to be baptized in the Holy Spirit with the exciting evidence of speaking in tongues, many people saw the meetings as a sign and wonder. The pastor, William J. Seymour, was a black man and the mission staff and congregation were completely integrated. Indeed, as Frank Bartleman famously said about Azusa Street, "The color line was washed away in the Blood." For a short time, interracial worship was widely accepted in the exploding Pentecostal churches around the nation.[5]

However, the color line reappeared as new denominations were formed, largely based on race. The Assemblies of God was formed in 1914 by white ministers, most of whom had been part of the Church of God in Christ, which was led by a black bishop, Charles H. Mason. Other Pentecostal churches continued to divide on the basis of race, and until 1924, the movement was almost totally divided between mostly black denominations and mostly white denominations.

In the mid-1940s, a movement toward unity occurred between white Pentecostal denominations that had drifted apart before World War II and now longed for a more united front as the nation faced the uncertainties of the postwar world. They were also concerned about the rise of the liberal-leaning National Council of Churches (NCC). These Pentecostal denominations had earlier joined the National Association of Evangelicals (NAE) to fight for freedom to air their own radio broadcasts without government restrictions.

In 1948, the white Pentecostal denominations formed the Pentecostal Fellowship of North America (PFNA) as a sign of unity to the church world. This unity, however, didn't include black Pentecostal churches, which were not invited to join. Even though my father was a leader in forming both the NAE and the PFNA, I was mostly unaware of these developments. In the end, although the Pentecostals claimed to be "saved, sanctified and filled with the Holy Ghost," they were no different than other church traditions in America when it came to race.[6]

Some Pentecostal leaders explained that racially separated churches could evangelize their own people better than mixed churches could. But the contradiction of sending hundreds of missionaries to evangelize Africa while doing nothing for blacks in their own backyards began to take its toll. A younger generation of ministers began to wonder why a movement that started out with racial unity had grown so far apart. Also, with the advent of the civil rights movement in the 1960s, many Pentecostals longed to be free from the chains of injustice and separation from their fellow Pentecostal brothers and sisters in black churches. The lines were drawn between the older generation of white leaders who saw no problems with segregated churches and the younger generation who grew up after the 1954 *Brown vs. Board of Education* decision, which integrated the nation's public schools.

Charismatic Unity

The advent of the charismatic movement in 1960 and the creation of the Society for Pentecostal Studies (SPS), which I helped to found in 1970, brought more contacts between black and white Pentecostals. The congresses sponsored by the North American Renewal Service Committee (NARSC) in the 1980s and 90s also brought many black and white Pentecostal leaders together for the first time as they served on the steering committee to plan massive charismatic rallies in New Orleans, Indianapolis, St. Louis and Orlando.

While I didn't realize it at the time, I ended up playing a role in breaking down the system that I now call "Pentecostal Jim Crowism." In the great Kansas City conference of 1977, I served as the chairman of the Pentecostal track, while Kevin Ranaghan led the Catholic charismatics and Larry Christenson led the mainline Protestant charismatics. Because there were so many black Pentecostal leaders and so few black charismatic leaders, the committee asked me to recruit as many black leaders as possible. In a short time, I was able to persuade the presiding bishop of the Church of God in Christ, J. O. Patterson, to serve as a main speaker, as well as Jim Forbes from the United Holy Church. Serving on the planning committee were Bishops Samuel Green and Ithiel Clemmons, who were also from the Church of God in Christ.[7]

After the Kansas City conference, when I was chosen to lead these groups in planning other major conferences, I made even more efforts to include black speakers and musicians. All of this resulted in the formation of the North America Renewal Service Committee (NARSC) in 1985. This group was made up of all denominational groups including Catholic and Protestant charismatics and both black and white Pentecostal denominations. In the planning sessions for these conferences I invited Bernard Underwood from my own church to serve on the planning committee. In the many planning sessions leading up to the New Orleans Congress of 1987, Clemmons and Underwood became fast friends. In the end, they together envisioned and planned for the famous "Memphis Miracle" that took place in 1994.

The Architects of Unity

The process began in 1991, when Underwood was elected to head the Pentecostal Fellowship of North America (PFNA). At that time, he purposed in his heart to use his term to end the racial divide between the Pentecostal churches. On March 6, 1992, the PFNA's board of administration voted unanimously to "pursue the possibility of reconciliation with our African American brethren." After this, four important meetings took place.

The first meeting was on July 31, 1992, in Dallas, Texas, in the DFW Hyatt Regency Hotel, where Church of God in Christ bishop O. T. Jones captivated the PFNA leaders with his wit and wisdom.

The second meeting was held in Phoenix, Arizona, on January 4–5, 1993, where Church of God in Christ pastor Reuben Anderson from Compton, California (representing Bishop Charles Blake), played a key role in explaining the challenges of urban ministries in America.

The third key meeting convened at the PFNA annual meeting in Atlanta, Georgia, on October 25–27, 1993. Jack Hayford, of the International Church of the Foursquare Gospel, and Bishop Gilbert Patterson, of the Church of God in Christ, strongly affirmed the plans for reconciliation.

A fourth meeting in Memphis, Tennessee, in January 1994, became known as the "20/20 meeting" because twenty white leaders and twenty black leaders joined to plan the climactic conference being planned for October 1994 in Memphis. The goal was for the old PFNA to be laid to rest in order to birth a new fellowship without racial or ethnic boundaries.

With the unanimous support of the member bodies, Underwood and Clemmons took up the two-year process of dismantling the PFNA and constructing a new interracial organization. I was asked by the leaders to serve as chairman of a committee to draw up a constitution for the new and as-yet-unnamed group. As chairman, I worked with many denominational leaders in drafting the document, and I was amazed at the practical unanimity on all the points we put into the document.

Our first decision was to scrap the old PFNA entirely and create a totally new organization. The name we chose was Pentecostal Churches of North America (PCNA). For the first few years, we decided that the group would operate with two cochairmen, one black and one white. We came to Memphis in the fall of 1994 with high expectations.

The Memphis Miracle

October 18, 1994, was a day never to be forgotten in the annals of American Pentecostalism—a date when the Holy Spirit moved in Memphis to end decades of racial separation and open doors to a new era of cooperation and fellowship between African American and white Pentecostals. At the time, it was called the "Memphis Miracle" by those gathered in Memphis as well as in the national press, which hailed the historic importance of the event.[8]

When the delegates arrived in Memphis on October 17, 1994, they sensed an electric air of expectation that something wonderful was about to happen. The conference theme was "Pentecostal Partners: A Reconciliation Strategy for 21st Century Ministry." More than three thousand people attended the evening sessions in the Dixon-Meyers Hall of the Cook Convention Center in downtown Memphis. Most people attending were aware of the racial strife in Memphis where Martin Luther King Jr. had been assassinated in 1968. The hope was for a great racial healing to take place. The evening services reflected the tremendous work done by the local committee in the months before the gathering. Bishop Gilbert Patterson of the Temple of Deliverance Church of God in Christ, and Samuel Middlebrook, pastor of the Raleigh Assembly of God in Memphis, cochaired the committee. Although both men had pastored in the same city for 29 years, they'd never met. The Memphis meetings brought them together.

The morning sessions were remarkable for the honesty and candor of the papers presented by a team of leading Pentecostal scholars. These included Dr. Cecil M. Robeck Jr. of Fuller Theological Seminary and the Assemblies of God, Dr. Leonard Lovett of the Church of God in Christ and Dr. William Turner of Duke University and the United Holy Church. Because I was also one of the main speakers, I recounted the sad history of racial separation and compromise that had marred the otherwise mighty Pentecostal movement and called for what I called a "miracle in Memphis" to bring an end to this dark era of our history. In these sessions, the sad history of separation, racism and neglect was laid bare before the one thousand or more assembled delegates. These sometimes chilling confessions brought a stark sense of past injustice and the absolute need for repentance and reconciliation. The evening worship sessions were full of Pentecostal fire and fervor as Bishop G. E. Patterson, Billy Joe Daugherty and Jack Hayford preached rousing sermons to the receptive crowds.[9]

The climactic moment, however, came in the scholars' session on the afternoon of October 18, after bishop Blake tearfully told the delegates, "Brothers and sisters, I commit my love to you. There are problems down the road, but a strong commitment to love will overcome them all." Suddenly a sweeping move of the Holy Spirit came over the entire assembly. A young black man uttered a spirited message in tongues after which Jack Hayford hurried to the microphone to give the interpretation. He began by saying, "For the Lord would speak to you this day, by the tongue, by the quickening of the Spirit, and He would say":

> My sons and My daughters, look if you will from the heavenward side of things, and see where you have been—two, separate streams, that is, streams as at flood tide. For I have poured out of My Spirit upon you and flooded you with grace in both your circles of gathering and fellowship. But as streams at flood tide, nonetheless, the waters have been muddied to some degree. Those of desperate thirst have come, nonetheless, for muddy water is better than none at all.
>
> My sons and My daughters, if you will look and see that there are some not come to drink because of what they have seen. You have not been aware of it, for only heaven has seen those who would doubt what flowed in your midst, because of the waters muddied having been soiled by the clay of your humanness, not by your crudity, lucidity or intentionality, but by the clay of your humanness the river has been made impure.
>
> But look. Look, for I, by My Spirit, am flowing the two streams into one. And the two becoming one, if you can see from the heaven side of things, are being purified and not only is there a new purity coming in your midst, but there will be multitudes more who will gather at this one mighty river because they will see the purity of the reality of My love manifest in you. And so, know that as heaven observes and tells us what is taking place there is reason for you to rejoice and prepare yourself, for here shall be multitudes more than ever before come to this joint surging of My grace among you, says the Lord.[10]

Immediately, a white pastor appeared in the wings of the backstage with a towel and a basin of water. His name was Donald Evans, an Assemblies of God pastor from Tampa, Florida. When he explained that the Lord had called him to wash the feet of a black leader as a sign of repentance, he was given access to the platform. In a moment of tearful contrition, he washed the feet of Bishop Clemmons while begging forgiveness for the sins of white people against their black brothers and sisters. A wave of weeping swept over the auditorium. Then, Blake approached Thomas Trask, General Superintendent of the Assemblies of God, and tearfully washed his feet as a sign of repentance for any animosity black people had harbored against their white brothers and sisters. This was the climactic moment of the conference. We all sensed that this was the final seal of approval from the heart of God over the proceedings. In an emotional speech the next day, Dr. Paul Walker of the Church of God (Cleveland, Tennessee) also called this event "The Memphis Miracle," a name that struck and made headlines around the world.

That afternoon, the members of the old PFNA gathered for the final session of its history. In a very short session, a motion was carried to dissolve the old, all-white organization in favor of a new entity that would be birthed the next day. But more reconciliation was yet to come!

I was chosen to preside over the session where the constitution for the new organization was adopted. For me, this was a *kairos* moment as I recalled that, in 1948, my father had been active in forming the PFNA. Now a new generation faced the bewildering problems that our forefathers weren't willing to face.

When the new constitution was read to the delegates on October 19, a new name was proposed for the group, "Pentecostal Churches of North America" (PCNA). We agreed that the governing board of the new group have equal numbers of black and white leaders and that denominational charter memberships would be welcomed that very day. However, before the constitution came before the assembly for a vote,

Pastor Billy Joe Daugherty of Tulsa's Victory Christian Center asked the delegates to include the word "charismatic" in the new name. Over a hastily called luncheon meeting of the restructuring committee, we agreed that Christians who thought of themselves as charismatics would also be invited to join. When the vote was taken, the body unanimously voted to call the new organization the "Pentecostal and Charismatic Churches of North America" (PCCNA). As a result, the Memphis Miracle not only included the beginning of healing between black and white Pentecostals, but also between Pentecostals and charismatics.

Another issue surfaced when a pastor from the Pentecostal Assemblies of the World asked why the non-Trinitarian or "Oneness" Pentecostals weren't invited to join. The response was swift, as Trinitarian delegates spoke in no uncertain terms that this wasn't the time or place nor the proper forum to debate that issue, the most fundamental theological split in the history of the movement. As chairman, I feared that the entire conference might fall apart if this issue hit the floor. Our major purpose in Memphis was to heal the racial divide, not to heal theological divides. With a heavy heart, we went on and adopted the constitution without the participation of the Oneness brothers and sisters, many of whom were black. Looking back, I have wondered if we missed a historic opportunity to settle this issue also on that historic day.

Another milestone of the day was the unanimous adoption of a "Racial Reconciliation Manifesto" drafted by Bishop Ithiel Clemmons, Dr. Cecil M. Robeck Jr., Dr. Leonard Lovett and Dr. Harold D. Hunter. In this historic document, the new PCCNA pledged to "oppose racism prophetically in all its various manifestations" and to be "vigilant in the struggle." The organization's members further agreed to "confess that racism is a sin and as a blight must be condemned" while promising to "seek partnerships and exchange pulpits with persons of a different hue . . . in the spirit of our Blessed Lord who prayed that we might be one."[11]

After this, the election of officers took place with Bishop Clemmons chosen as chairman and Bishop Underwood as vice chairman. Also elected to the board was Bishop Barbara Amos, whose election demonstrated the resolve of the new organization to bridge the gender gap as well. The other officers represented a balance of black and white leaders from the constituent membership.

Subsequent meetings of the PCCNA, especially in Memphis in 1996 and Washington, D.C. in 1997, showed that the road to racial reconciliation in America wouldn't be short or easy. But at Memphis in 1994, the road ahead was made much easier as the American Pentecostals attempted to put away this dark chapter of their history. I was honored and happy to be a part of this historic moment in American church history.

In the very years that these memorable events were taking place to begin a new day in race relations, newer revivals broke out in Toronto and Pensacola that I believe might have been spiritually related to the events in Memphis. But that is another story.

10

Toronto, Brownsville and Lakeland Revivals

One of the strongest currents in the colorful history of American religious life has been the sudden appearance of revivals that brought new life and new converts into the churches. These spiritual awakenings have sporadically occurred at various points in the life of most Protestant traditions. Church historians have given names to some of these unusual movings of the Spirit, often calling them "great awakenings."

Great Awakenings

The "First Great Awakening" began in Massachusetts under the spellbinding preaching of Jonathan Edwards. From 1736 to 1740, the stern Puritans in his Congregational church in Northampton were emotionally stirred by sermons such as "Sinners in the Hands of an Angry God." People cried out for mercy, fell out in the Spirit, wept in abject repentance and shouted loudly when they "prayed through" to deliverance. Following Edwards, the English Methodist evangelist George Whitefield came to America and eventually preached to huge crowds in all the colonies. Called the "Heavenly Comet," Whitefield was an orator without peer.[1]

What was called the "Second Great Awakening" occurred in the Cane Ridge camp meeting in the backwoods of frontier Kentucky in 1801, in meetings led by Presbyterians, Methodists and Baptists. Under the leadership of Presbyterian pastor Barton Stone, crowds of 25,000 gathered in what became the first camp meeting in American history. The frenzy of worshipers shouting, weeping and howling in repentance was so loud that some compared the sound to the "noise of Niagara." Many unusual manifestations began to occur in the highly charged services. Some people fell out in the Spirit, others got the "jerks," others shouted at the top of their lungs, while others ran into the forest barking like dogs, trying to "tree the devil." Barton called them the falling, running, dancing, shouting, singing and barking "exercises." In his autobiography published in 1849, he called them "genuine works of God," despite four decades of criticism.[2]

The "Third Great Awakening" came in 1858, just three years before the outbreak of the Civil War. Starting as a noon prayer meeting in the fish markets on Fulton Street in New York City, the prayer movement spread across the nation in a matter of weeks. Someone called it the "two-thousand-mile prayer meeting," which stretched from New York City to Omaha. The movement soon spread to England where similar meetings dotted the English landscape. In all, some historians have estimated that more than a million souls were converted and added to the churches in this memorable time of refreshing. Sadly, this revival didn't reach into the American South, which had sunken into the pits of defending slavery rather than looking for revival.[3]

Some historians speak of the Azusa Street Revival of 1906–1909 as the "Fourth Great Awakening." More than a million Pentecostal congregations were brought into being around the world as a result of this historic revival. Also proceeding from the Pentecostal movement was the charismatic renewal movement; it began in 1960 and extended the "Holy Spirit Renewal" to both Protestant and Catholic mainline churches in all parts of the world.[4]

In 1948, four decades later, a renewal within Pentecostalism came with the advent of the Latter Rain Movement, which began in Sharon Bible College, a Pentecostal school in Saskatchewan, Manitoba. Spreading rapidly to the United States, this movement emphasized abundant tongues, prophecies, healings and the laying on of hands to "impart" specific gifts. "Singing in the Spirit" (tongues) by entire congregations was a new phenomenon that became widespread. In addition, teachers in the Latter Rain Movement emphasized the restoration of the "five-fold ministries" (apostles, prophets, evangelists, pastors and teachers). At the same time, more radical teachers spoke of the appearance of the "manifested sons of God" who would be supernaturally empowered to take part in the last revival just before the sudden Second Coming of Christ and the Rapture of the Church. This revival, although rejected by Pentecostal denominations, continued to influence many people. This influence extended to the earliest leaders of the Catholic charismatic movement, which began in 1967 in Pittsburgh, Pennsylvania.[5]

As time goes on, the charismatic renewal might be seen by future historians as the "Fifth Great Awakening," because it also included the Jesus Movement, which swept through a whole generation of young people, most of whom were charismatics.

A cursory look at the aforementioned revivals shows that they usually came in roughly fifty-year cycles (1740s, 1801, 1858, 1901–1909, 1948). Interestingly, the Toronto and Brownsville revivals also fit into this pattern, beginning around 1994 and extending through most of the 1990s.

The Toronto Blessing Revival

What became known as the "Toronto Blessing" started in January 1994, in the Toronto Airport Vineyard, a church led by John and Carol Arnott. This congregation was part of the Vineyard Movement founded by John Wimber with headquarters in California. The Toronto Airport Vineyard consisted of some three hundred members and was located near the Toronto airport, which accounts for its name.

The revival started as an offshoot of the "Laughing Revivals" led by Rodney Howard Brown, a Pentecostal evangelist from South Africa. The catalyst for the Toronto meetings was the preaching of another Vineyard pastor, Randy Clark from St. Louis. After hearing Brown and being slain in the Spirit several times, Clark was invited by Arnott to come for four days of renewal services at the Airport Vineyard. The four days stretched into weeks as people heard what was going on in Toronto. During these meetings, people laughed uncontrollably, fell out in the Spirit, rolled on the floor and copiously wept as they experienced the power of the Holy Spirit. Arnott called it a spiritual "party" where "people would become so empowered that emotional hurts from childhood would just fall off." All of these manifestations were common in John Wimber's services. So, in a sense, Toronto was at first a typical Vineyard church.[6]

After months of meetings with people coming from all over the world, studies were done about those who came. A surprisingly large number were "burned-out Pentecostals," both clergy and laypersons, who came for a "refreshing" in the Spirit. However, some Pentecostals were critical of the Toronto meetings, because speaking in tongues wasn't emphasized and seldom was heard in the meetings.

As time went on, the Toronto Vineyard developed a type of liturgy to minister to the huge numbers of people who came expecting a spiritual overhaul. Usually, after a long time of worship with guitars, tambourines and drums, Arnott or a visiting preacher would deliver a sermon generally defending the revival and the manifestations. During the sermons, it wasn't unusual for hundreds of people in the audience to begin laughing uproariously, to run around the sanctuary or to weep loudly.

After the sermons, all the chairs would be stacked in the corners and inside the walls of the church with a call for ministers and "catchers" to come forward. Duct-taped lines were already taped on the floors, and as seekers came forward and lined up dozens of rows deep, those who ministered stood on one side of the line laying hands on them and praying for more of the Spirit. Almost all of them fell out "slain in the Spirit," were caught by the catchers and were gently lowered to the floor where "modesty cloths" were usually spread over the legs of women who were out in the Spirit. Many people testified to receiving marvelous physical or inner healing, as well as experiencing dreams and visions.

As time went on, however, more exotic manifestations began to occur that raised concerns at Wimber's headquarters in California. These included people making animal noises, such as barking like dogs, roaring like lions and crowing like chickens. In a short time, the Toronto meetings began to overshadow Wimber and the rest of the Vineyard movement as many articles appeared in *Christianity Today* and *Charisma* magazines. Religious news services and even the secular press ran vivid stories both pro and con about the revival. As typically happens, the extensive press coverage caused thousands of people around the world to pray for the revival to come to their own local churches. By the end of 1995, an estimated six hundred thousand visitors had flown to Toronto from all over the world to see and experience for themselves the now famous Toronto revival. Because the original church building seated only four hundred people and couldn't hold the crowds, a new sanctuary of more than three thousand seats was hastily secured.

During this time, I was interviewed about the Toronto manifestations by many newspapers, magazines and television shows like the *700 Club*. I was seen as a historian who could speak knowledgeably about such things. My explanations were always that these types of manifestations had been common throughout much of American religious history. I usually referred to the Cane Ridge camp meetings, the Holiness movement and the Pentecostal movement. In fact, I would note that I'd seen just about all of these manifestations in my childhood, growing up in red-hot Pentecostal revivals and camp meetings. I was generally positive, seeing in the Toronto meetings a continuation of the classical Pentecostal movement.[7]

At about this time, an Assemblies of God evangelist, Steve Hill, visited the Holy Trinity Church in Brompton, a charismatic Anglican church near London pastored by Sandy Miller. Before Hill arrived, the church had experienced falling in the Spirit and other types of Pentecostal demonstrations. With Hill's ministry, many of the same radical Toronto manifestations began to occur in the old Brompton church. Because the media was saturated with reports of the Toronto meetings, some London newspapers dubbed the manifestations as the "Toronto Blessing." The name stuck and all over the world the revival was referred to as the Toronto Blessing rather than the Vineyard Revival. In fact, for a short time Arnott was better known than John Wimber in the charismatic world.

To some observers, the Toronto movement was becoming larger than the entire Vineyard movement. In response to the idea of a "Toronto Blessing," in 1995 Arnott published a book with the title *The Father's Blessing*. Interestingly, John Wimber endorsed the book with a favorable blurb on the back cover. In his advice to Arnott, Wimber counseled the Toronto pastor not to stop the manifestations, but he clearly warned him not to "platform" them or to "theologize" about them.

As the Toronto meetings continued, however, all was not well between Wimber and Arnott. Even though he endorsed Arnott's book, Wimber increasingly rejected the Toronto revival in general and the "exotic manifestations" in particular. After carefully reading the book *The Father's Blessing*, Wimber felt that Arnott had failed to follow his counsel. He determined to expel the Toronto church from the Vineyard fellowship, largely because he was dealing with so many calls about Toronto, he was able to do little else but deal with the manifestations that he clearly felt were harming the reputation of the Vineyard movement.

About this time, Wimber called several leaders to get their advice on his plans to expel the church, and I was among those he called. I remember a very long phone call where Wimber laid out the problem to me and asked if he was doing the right thing in the light of previous history. While I agreed that the manifestations were indeed "exotic," I told him that they had occurred in previous historic revivals and were really nothing new. I then counseled him not to excommunicate the church because, in my opinion, such radical manifestations usually didn't last long and would probably soon disappear. He would be losing the one congregation that more than any other was spreading the Vineyard movement around the world. In other words, he would lose more than he would gain.

In spite of my advice, Wimber flew to Toronto in December 1995 and disfellowshiped Arnott and his church from the Vineyard movement. Soon after this, Arnott reorganized his church and renamed it the Toronto Airport Christian Fellowship. From the very beginnings, this new denomination was quite large, with churches joining from all over the world.

Not long after this, Arnott invited me to speak in the annual pastors' conference of the new fellowship. Because I hadn't been one of those who flocked to Toronto while it was in the Vineyard, it was an opportunity for me to see the revival close up. When I arrived for the first service, I sat on the front row beside Carol Arnott. Many people came to her for private prayer. As the service continued with lively singing, I saw a man lying on his back behind the pulpit. He was twitching and laughing. Later, he came and sat beside me. I looked up and recognized him as Clark Pinnock, the famous evangelical scholar. This was indeed surprising to me.

On this night, my friend Dr. Margaret Paloma was the main speaker. I'd known her for years as an astute sociologist from the University of Akron in Ohio. She was a close follower of all things Pentecostal and charismatic and a very strong advocate of the Toronto revival. When she was introduced to speak, a holy pandemonium broke out all over the church. Hundreds of people began to scream, shout, weep and run around the building. The sound was deafening. Arnott stood behind Paloma as she tried to speak above the din. The people seemed to know that they had permission to release all the demonstrations they were longing to express.

It was an amazing night. Although it looked as if confusion reigned, I did perceive that the Holy Spirit was at work and that many people were rejoicing over spiritual victories they were receiving in Toronto.

The next night, I was the main speaker. The crowd was much more subdued and listened to every word as I spoke. The relative calm made me wonder if I had the proper anointing for this kind of service. At the end, I led the thousands of people in an impassioned Korean-style loud and sustained concert prayer, which lasted about fifteen minutes. It was one of the highlights of my ministry. While there, I was interviewed on Canadian national television and gave a positive account of the revival. Arnott then asked me to serve as an advisor to him and the Toronto Airport Christian Fellowship.

The Brownsville Revival

Soon after the Toronto revival began to peak, a similar revival broke out in the large Brownsville Assemblies of God congregation near Pensacola, Florida. For months in early 1995, pastor John Kilpatrick led his flock in earnest prayers for revival.

According to members of the church, Kilpatrick's wife, Brenda, had flown to Toronto where she received healing of a long-standing back problem. Later, she took the entire church staff to Arnott's church in Toronto, which provides a possible link between the two revivals.

On Father's Day, June 18, 1995, a monumental revival broke out under the preaching of Kilpatrick's friend, Steve Hill, who happened to be visiting him at the time. Again, Hill had ministered at the Brompton, England, Anglican church that experienced a Toronto Blessing–type revival. That day, hundreds of people refused to leave the church after an altar call brought a thousand people to the front to seek salvation. Then strange manifestations began to occur, similar to those in Toronto. Many people fell out in the Spirit, while others shook violently or wept openly. Hill was asked to stay and continue the services. Every night for many months, thousands of people crowded into the church, with some crowds reaching five thousand people. In a short time, the Brownsville revival surpassed the Toronto revival in visitors and converts.

Interestingly, Steve Hill was born in Turkey. In his younger days, he had been a roistering drug addict and alcoholic. This all changed when a Lutheran vicar prayed for him and he received a dramatic conversion and total deliverance from his addictions. After attending David Wilkerson's Twin Oaks Academy in Texas, Hill visited Argentina, where he saw the massive crusades of Carlos Anacondia and Claudio Freidzon. After helping plant several churches in Argentina, he returned to the United States to become a leading evangelist in the Assemblies of God.

Since the Brownsville services were held in an Assemblies of God church, the revival was more in line with traditional Pentecostal revivals. The preachers gave altar calls for salvation and people received baptism in the Holy Spirit with tongues as evidence. People also experienced divine healing. As the services continued week after week, young high school students carried the revival to their schools—to the consternation of some school administrators. So many teenagers and young adults were converted that the church opened a Bible school, the Brownsville Revival School of Ministry, which soon grew to more than a thousand students.

At this time I was dean of the School of Divinity at Regent University in Virginia Beach, Virginia, a school founded by Pat Robertson. The Toronto and Brownsville revivals were the talk of both faculty and students. Some even flew to Toronto and Pensacola to receive a "new touch" from the Lord. One of our newly minted graduates in the M.A. program, Steve Ault, became so excited that he decided to take his family and move to Brownsville to teach in the new school. He went with no invitation and no offer of a job. However, soon after arriving, the school president, Michael Brown, hired him to teach New Testament and Greek. In a short time, Ault had as many as six hundred students in each class.

In time, Brown divided the school when the Assemblies of God pressured him to make the school into an Assemblies of God institution. Despite such educational problems, the revival continued throughout the 1990s. At the height of the meetings, lines formed several hours in advance with people who wanted to get inside the church. Several thousand who couldn't get in were seated in tents with closed-circuit television. To feed the crowds, as many as eight trucks served food to the people, who experienced physical as well as spiritual hunger.

Unlike the Toronto revival where the Vineyard denomination expelled the local congregation, the Brownsville revival received the blessing of the Assemblies of God leadership. Instead of featuring and defending the more exotic manifestations, Hill centered his ministry on the altar calls for salvation of the unconverted or for the restoration of backsliders who had fallen away from the faith. The services also featured passionate preaching from Hill, Kilpatrick and others who were invited to speak.

Although I didn't attend the Brownsville revival services, again I was asked to comment on the meetings in magazines, newspapers and television interviews. In the St. Louis charismatic conference that I led in 2000, some eighteen thousand people registered from all the different churches. Again, half of the participants were Roman Catholics. I invited Steve Hill to give the altar call on the final night. It was an awesome sight as many thousands came forward to repeat the sinner's prayer for salvation. Others came forward to rededicate their lives, or to seek healing or deliverance from addictions. It was one of the most passionate and effective altar calls I'd ever seen in my life.[8]

The Lakeland Revival

A third revival similar to the Toronto and Brownsville revivals occurred in 2008 in Lakeland, Florida. This was the first revival in America that was carried nightly for months on live television to a nationwide audience with millions of potential viewers. Lakeland had witnessed a charismatic revival in the 1980s in the Carpenters Home Church pastored by Karl Strader. He had built a church that seated ten thousand people, and the city was also the home of Southeastern Assemblies of God University, where hundreds of young students prepared for Pentecostal ministry. Steve Strader, the son of Karl Strader, worked with his father for years in the church and in its extensive radio ministry. By 2008, he had left his father's ministry and founded his own congregation, which he called the "Ignite Church."

I'd known Karl Strader for many years as one of the leaders of the charismatic movement. I'd preached in his cavernous church several times. Although he pastored the largest Assemblies of God church in Florida, some believed he veered too far in the direction of nondenominational charismatic worship. I'd also known Steve Strader for many years, and I saw him as an enthusiastic young man with a passion to be on the cutting edge of any revival movement that came along. They were a great father-and-son team.

In April 2008, Steve Strader invited a Canadian evangelist, Todd Bentley, from Abbottsburg, British Columbia, to come to his Ignite Church in Lakeland for a five-day revival. Once started, the revival went on for months and ended in October 2008. The six months of services attracted tens of thousands of visitors from all parts of the world. This was the beginning of one of the most colorful and controversial series of revival meetings in the history of the United States.

Bentley was the most unlikely evangelist that could be imagined. As a teenager, he had not only abused drugs and alcohol, but had been part of what he called a "sexual assault ring" that molested children. In these wild days, he had placed tattoos over large parts of his body. For the rest of his life, the way he dressed suggested that he had just come out of a bar. But at the age of eighteen, he was converted to Pentecostal Christianity and began a ministry where he gave testimony to his wayward past and to his miraculous conversion.

In 1998, he spoke to an evangelistic group in Abbottsburg, called "Fresh Fire Ministries." The leaders were so impressed that they immediately made Bentley the head of the group so they could support his worldwide ministry. His ministry of healing was patterned after the famous English Pentecostal evangelist Smith Wigglesworth, who would often punch people in the stomach and sometimes knock them over as he prayed for their healing.

In advertising the meetings in Lakeland, Strader used many modern media techniques, including webcasts, live streaming services on the web and ultimately live cable television. God TV preempted its other programming to broadcast the services live nightly during the week. People all over the world tuned in for hours each evening to watch the exotic music, light shows and Bentley's unorthodox methods of praying for the sick. The attendance in Strader's church soon ballooned until they had to move several times to larger and larger facilities. When they moved to the Lakeland Center and Marchant Stadium, at a cost of fifteen thousand dollars per night, the attendance increased to the thousands. In the end, they rented a tent where attendance peaked at around ten thousand people per night. Although I never attended a live service, as many of my friends did, I did see the revival up close on television.

What I saw on God TV was a huge crowd of people from all over the world who flocked to Lakeland to receive healing and a new touch from God. In many ways, the meetings resembled the Toronto meetings, with many manifestations taking place in the audience. But the center of attention was always on the platform and especially on Bentley. Often he would shake his head, shout at a seeker and often punch the individual in the stomach or side in a violent attempt to drive out sickness or demons that he explained also caused diseases. On TV, I didn't observe the fully developed sermons or biblical teachings that were so common in Toronto and Brownsville. In spite of the tattooed preacher and his unorthodox methods, thousands of spiritually hungry people from all walks of life came forward for healing prayers.

Unlike Toronto and Brownsville, the Lakeland revival lasted only a few months—from April to October 2008—when the services ceased and many converts moved on to Steve Strader's Ignite Church. One reason for the decline was criticism that appeared in Christian magazines, in newspapers and even on national network television. Bentley was criticized for yelling "Bam, Bam" before punching the seekers, for claiming that twenty people had been raised from the dead and for saying that he had talked with an angel named Emma. Soon, MSNBC showed a critical clip from the revival, and things began to go downhill. The final blow came in August

2008 when Bentley announced that he was separating from his wife. As attendance went down, the meetings returned to Strader's Ignite Church, where it all began only six months before.

Although I didn't attend the Lakeland services, as I watched the meetings on TV, I sensed that little scriptural foundation was given in the meetings. Also, something didn't ring true about Bentley's frenetic ministry. I'm sure that many people were converted and healed during the revival. But in the end, the revival seemed to cast a pall over similar revivals that might break out in the future. In the end, my sense is that the Toronto and Brownsville revivals, which were practically simultaneous in time, could well go down in history as parts of another great awakening in the style of the Cane Ridge and Azusa Street revivals. The Lakeland revival, in all probability, will be seen as a footnote to the first two.

While the Toronto, Brownsville and Lakeland revivals dominated headlines, another movement known as the "New Apostolic Reformation" was developing among non-denominational Pentecostals and charismatics that would eventually capture the attention of the church world. I was to play a small role in discerning the features of this developing movement.

11

The New Apostolic Reformation Movement

During the 1980s, increasing discussion and debate took place among some Pentecostals and independent charismatics over the question of restoring the office of apostle to the modern church.

I sensed a growing impatience among church leaders with the power of the laity in some local churches, which sometimes limited the effectiveness of pastors who had been "sent by God" and anointed to the office of pastor. Often, a prominent family exercised almost autocratic control over a local church and sent pastors packing before they could establish a successful ministry. This led to a growing sense that nothing should inhibit the anointed work of the man of God, especially any obstinate laypersons who tried to control the congregation.

Added to this discussion was a backlog of teachings on the "five-fold ministries" from the Latter Rain Movement of the 1940s and 1950s, which called for more power at the top of both denominations and local churches. This led to a renewed emphasis on the prophetic and apostolic ministries that gained in popularity as the 1980s came to an end.

I was suddenly brought into the discussion on modern apostles at an annual meeting of the "Idea Exchange" in Orlando, Florida, in January 1989. This meeting, led by Karl Strader and Quinton Edwards, was a forum for pastors of churches with more than a thousand members. As I recall, more than four hundred pastors and other church leaders attended the first session of the meeting. Before I could find a seat, I heard Strader calling me to the platform as an "expert" on church history to discuss the question, "Are there apostles today?" I had to formulate my answer on the way to the microphone.

I essentially said, "Yes, there are modern apostles, but not the way many people think." I stated that the twelve original disciples of Jesus constituted a unique group of apostles that would never be repeated. But in my studies of church history, after the original Twelve had died, the church used the word "apostle" mainly to refer to missionaries who brought the Gospel for the first time to unreached peoples who had never before heard the message. The examples I gave were St. Patrick, the "apostle to Ireland"; Cyrill and Methodius, the "apostles to the Slavs"; and St. Augustine of Canterbury, the "apostle to Britain." Although other uses existed for the word "apostle," the missionary function was the highest and most accepted use in the long history of the Church.

This explanation didn't go over well with the crowd, because many attending thought of themselves as modern-day apostles, yet they didn't qualify in the way I'd defined the term. Some even stood up and stated that they believed they were apostles. Strader then asked for all who considered themselves to be apostles to stand. I counted as exactly twelve pastors stood and claimed the title. I knew some of them and, although they were wonderful men, I certainly did not see them as apostles.

Two years after the Idea Exchange meetings, I was invited by *Ministries Today* magazine to write an article titled "Who Are the Modern Apostles?" The article appeared in the March–April 1992 issue. I did a great deal of research for this article and learned a lot about the history of apostles throughout church history from the beginning to the present day. I learned that the original twelve apostles never ordained new apostles, just bishops and elders. However, several people beyond the original Twelve in the New Testament were called apostles. Among them were Andronicus and Junia, who was probably a woman apostle.

The Roman Church eventually settled on the formula that bishops were the "successors of the apostles," and that they exercised the authority handed down from the Twelve. To be sure, in the ensuing two hundred years, many travelers called themselves apostles and prophets as they continued to visit the churches. After the bishops consolidated their power, the last thing they wanted was a so-called apostle or prophet to visit their churches. It could be dangerous, for example, if an "apostle" exposed any sins or irregularities in a bishop's use of power. An insight to this situation was recorded in a passage in the *Didache*, the oldest documents of the church fathers after the completion of the New Testament (written about A.D. 50–150). The passage reads as follows:

> Now as regards apostles or prophets, act strictly according to the precept of the Gospel. Upon his arrival every apostle must be welcomed as the Lord; but he must not stay except one day. In case of necessity, however, he may stay the next day also; but if he stays three days, he is a false prophet. At

> his departure the apostle must receive nothing except food till the next night's lodging; but if he asks for money, he is a false prophet.[1]

As this shows, after a century or so, wandering apostles and prophets weren't taken seriously by the established church, and were seen as little more than traveling medicine men. Obviously, the bishops and elders had taken full control of the churches with no place left for apostles to wield any kind of authority.

On the other hand, many other people continued to be sent out as missionaries to unreached peoples around the Mediterranean world. They were often referred to as "apostles to . . . [their countries of pioneering ministry]."

In spite of the low esteem shown to those who claimed to be apostles, the idea of a continuing apostleship continued to surface sporadically throughout church history. For example, Mani of Persia (A.D. 216–274), founder of the Manichee sect in the third century, called himself the "Apostle of Light." He said he was the last apostle of Jesus Christ who would ever appear. Like Mani, whose dualistic religion was rejected by the Church as heretical, most people in Church history who claimed to be new apostles have been branded as heretics and excommunicated from the Church. In fact, Mohammad also claimed to be the last apostle and prophet for all time. Other so-called end-time apostles, such as the Irvingites in Britain and the Mormons in America, have appeared over the centuries. But these self-proclaimed apostles have been rejected by mainstream Christianity.

The Irvingite Apostles

In the aftermath of the bloody French Revolution (1789–1799), a group of British Bible scholars concluded that they were living in the last days. Among these scholars was Edward Irving, the popular pastor of the Regents Square Presbyterian Church, the largest congregation in London, and John Nelson Darby, leader of the Plymouth Brethren. In their studies of biblical prophecies, they concluded that the biblical signs of the last days included the return of the Jews to Palestine, the restoration of the gifts of the Spirit and the restoration of the "fourfold" offices of apostles, prophets, evangelists and pastor-teachers. In particular, they looked for examples of speaking in tongues as a sure sign of the last days.[2]

In 1830, these men heard of a group in Port Glasgow, Scotland, where tongues were appearing in abundance. When some from London went to investigate, they discovered Mary Campbell and the McDonald twins, James and George. After hearing them speak in tongues, the scholars were convinced that these were the genuine tongues that they'd been seeking. Later, when Mary Campbell was invited to attend Irving's church in London, she suddenly began to speak in tongues one Sunday morning, causing consternation in the church. Soon after, Irving and his friends left the church and began to have separate services in what they called the "Catholic Apostolic Church." In time, seven churches were formed in London under pastors who were called "angels." Irving was one of these pastors. They named their new denomination the "Christian Apostolic Church."

As this was happening, Irving began to develop a theology of speaking in tongues in which he called tongues "the crowning act of all" the gifts and the "root and stem" out of which all the others grew. He also associated tongues with what he called the "baptism in the Holy Spirit," following John Wesley and John Fletcher. In spite of Irving's adventurous theology, to his great despair, he never spoke in tongues. Moreover, many of the other gifts of the Spirit began to appear in the churches, with great emphasis on the gift of prophecy. As the churches grew, the leaders began to stress the reappearance of the office of apostle, because they believed that without living apostles, "the Holy Ghost had abandoned the church." By 1835, the group decided to appoint from among themselves twelve end-time apostles who would be the last-days equals to the New Testament Twelve. They claimed that before the last of them died, the Rapture of the Church would take place.

The twelve were made up of clergymen, lawyers, aristocrats, artists and merchants. Two were members of Parliament. They established their headquarters in the cathedral-like church in Albury, which had been built by the famous Henry Drummond. From there, they developed many liturgies from all the traditions of Christianity, recorded all prophecies and assigned the "apostles" to rule over twelve European nations such as Russia, Germany, England, France and Spain. Their idea of evangelization was for the apostles to write long "testimonies" to be read to the crowned heads of the nations where each was assigned. In time, they organized churches in most European nations. Growth was steady for a time, until one by one the apostles died. Because they decided not to name successor apostles, the church began a rapid decline when the last of the original twelve died in 1901.

The only place where the church survived in large numbers was in Germany, where church leaders broke the rules and named a new apostle after the death of the last original one. Today, the German Catholic Apostolic Church is the third-largest Christian denomination in Germany after Roman Catholics and Lutherans.

In the end, the Catholic Apostolic Church failed because it was too elitist and appealed mainly to the upper classes. It never reached the poor masses of British society. Their evangelization mostly took place to the crowned heads of state, after which they believed that those nations had been "evangelized." Although they had tongues and apostles, the movement hardly survived the first generation in Britain. In sum, the movement was a failure.

The Mormon Apostles

At the same time that the British Catholic Apostolic Church appeared in England, another group of tongue speakers with restored apostles appeared in the United States. The Mormon movement, under the leadership of Joseph Smith, originated in the 1830s after Smith claimed to find "golden plates" while digging in a mountainside near Palmyra, New York. He claimed to be led by an angel named "Moroni." Believing that the plates were written in hieroglyphics, he attempted to translate them by using glasses made of "urim and thummin." Smith refused to let anyone else see the plates, and he worked behind a curtain as he wrote the *Book of Mormon*, a supposed translation of the mysterious plates.[3]

He claimed that the book contained the records of the ten lost tribes of Israel. These tribes somehow came to America in antiquity, and after Columbus discovered America they were known as "Indians." In the text, written in the style of the King James Bible, Smith told the story of Jesus appearing to these lost tribes and setting up what was later called the "Church of Jesus Christ of Latter-day Saints."

Interestingly, when setting up the doctrines and rituals of the new church, Smith added books known as *The Pearl of Great Price* and *Doctrines and Covenants*. In the ceremonies of the church, Smith included a ritual of laying on of hands to receive the "baptism in the Holy Ghost," which was often accompanied by speaking in tongues. Smith himself was often heard speaking in tongues.

After leaving New York because of persecution, Smith and his followers moved west, first to Kirtland, Ohio, and then on to Missouri, where a temple was built in the city of Independence. Only baptized Mormons could enter this temple. When the building was dedicated in 1838, records state that a thousand elders stood and "spoke in tongues" to the amazement of the young children who had never heard the manifestation before.

In their efforts to proselytize Protestants, Mormons often visited Methodist camp meetings where, at times, a Mormon woman would interrupt the services by speaking in tongues. Then a Mormon elder would proclaim that the campers should join the Mormons since they were the only true church as witnessed by speaking in tongues. Usually, they were unceremoniously cast off the grounds.

The Mormons, however, were persecuted not for tongues but because of the practice of plural marriage, which Smith—the "prophet" of the movement—advocated and practiced. Because of persecution in Missouri, Smith led his followers to build a city in Nauvoo, Illinois. However, an angry mob there assassinated Smith and scattered his followers. The new leader, Brigham Young—who ended up having twenty-four wives—led the church members to the Utah territory in Mexico, where they built Salt Lake City. Young promulgated a theology of polygamy that became the unique hallmark of the church. Young also was a tongues speaker, sometimes preaching entire sermons in tongues with the help of a translator who had the "gift of interpretation."

As far as church governance was concerned, in 1835, Brigham Young instituted the "Quorum of the Twelve," which was also called the "Council of the Twelve Apostles," who served as the supreme leaders of the church. In 1847, Young added the "First Presidency," an office that he held as the supreme leader of the church and that he used to direct the twelve apostles. He also claimed the ministry of "prophet," who could receive "revelations" that became binding on all Mormons.

Throughout the following years, the twelve apostles guided the affairs of the church. Unlike the Irvingites, however, the Mormons became an extremely missionary-minded church, sending thousands of young Mormon men around the world to proselytize anyone they could find to join the "Latter-day Saints." They offered converts the hope of becoming gods and goddesses in the future life. In retrospect, the Latter-day Saints have perhaps been the most successful modern church to attempt to use "apostles" as the ruling authorities in the church.

Pentecostal Apostles

In the twentieth century, the Pentecostal movement emerged as the most important and fastest-growing movement that emphasized the restoration of all New Testament gifts of the Spirit and the ministries of apostle, prophet, evangelist, pastor and teacher. In fact, the earliest name chosen by the Pentecostal movement in America was "Apostolic Faith," a designation given by Charles Parham to his church in Topeka, Kansas. In 1901, modern Pentecostalism began at Parham's church, which placed emphasis on the baptism in the Holy Spirit as evidenced by speaking in tongues. Parham's student William J. Seymour chose the same name for his Azusa Street Mission in Los Angeles in 1906.

In this context, however, the words "Apostolic Faith" didn't signal a move to restore the office of apostle to the church. Parham, in fact, was extremely critical of any kind of church government, much less a highly centralized system with apostolic authority. Yet, some Pentecostal scholars refer to Parham as the "apostle of Pentecost." Seymour has also been called an apostle of Pentecost to the world.

In the years that followed the glory days at Azusa Street, Pentecostal missionaries traveled around the world preaching the Latter Rain message of a mighty "Holy Ghost outpouring" before the Second Coming of Christ. A new generation of Pentecostal "apostles" appeared, such as G. B. Cashwell, the "apostle to the south"; T. B. Barratt, the "apostle to Europe"; W. C. Hoover, the "apostle to Chile"; Ivan Voronaev, the "apostle to the Slavs"; and Luigi Francescon, the "apostle to Italy." Interestingly, they never claimed to be apostles. The term came from historians like myself.

Other early Pentecostal groups did actually claim to restore the office of apostle to the church. These included apostolic churches in Wales, New Zealand, Australia, Canada and the United States. In these churches, "apostles" (usually twelve) were duly elected and ordained just as with any other office in the church. Some of these continue to this day, with colleges of apostles that govern their denominations.

The New Order of the Latter Rain Movement, beginning in Saskatchewan, British Columbia, in 1948, also popularized the idea of a restoration of the "five-fold ministries." This, they said, was in preparation for the revelation of the "manifested sons company," which they claimed would rule and reign at the end of the church age. Prominent among this elite manifested sons group would be prophets and apostles. The Latter Rain Movement also included a sweeping call for a new restoration of the gifts of the Spirit. This emphasis also included the impartation of specific gifts by the laying on of hands. Although the movement was rejected by the major Pentecostal denominations—including the Assemblies of God, the Church of God and the Pentecostal Holiness Church—

some doctrines continued to persist for years. Among them was the teaching that end-time apostles would soon appear to signal the Rapture of the Church. By the 1990s, some pastors from Latter Rain backgrounds had written books predicting the restoration of the "office" of apostle in the church. One of these was David Cannistraci's book *Apostles and the Emerging Apostolic Movement.*[4] This book and others caught the eye of Peter Wagner, who was about to call for a major conference on what he called "the post-denominational Church." In his view, mainline denominations were no longer relevant in the modern world, while independent megachurches were on the cutting edge of church growth.

The New Apostolic Reformation

Since 1994, Peter Wagner has led what he calls the "New Apostolic Reformation Movement," which he claims is now sweeping the world as the new way leaders are "doing church."

This movement came out of a conference Wagner led at Fuller Theological Seminary in 1996 called the "National Symposium on the Post-Denominational Church." After years of studying church growth in the "postmodern age," Wagner concluded that the day of the historic denomination was rapidly coming to a close while a new generation of post-denominational churches was dawning. Before the conference could convene, however, many critics of the idea—including Jack Hayford—forced Wagner to choose a new name. He finally settled on the term New Apostolic Churches to describe what he called a "New Testament model of leadership," or "new wineskins for a new church age."

These new churches, which many scholars think are actually "pre-denominational movements," would have the following "new" features:

1. A new name (New Apostolic Reformation)
2. New authority structures (the leaders are called "apostles")
3. New leadership training (no seminaries—instead led by volunteers, homegrown staff, local Bible colleges, etc.)
4. New ministry focus ("vision driven" [toward the future] rather than "heritage driven" [toward the past])
5. New worship styles (keyboards, ministry teams, lifted hands, loud praise, overhead projectors, etc.)
6. New prayer forms (concert prayer, singing in the Spirit, etc.)
7. New financing ("finances are abundant, giving is expected . . . beneficial . . . cheerful")
8. New outreach (church planting, compassion for the poor, etc.)
9. New power orientation (openness to the Holy Spirit and gifts of the Spirit—healing, demonic deliverance, prophecy, etc.)[5]

In his book describing this movement, *The New Apostolic Churches*, Wagner listed eighteen pastors (or "apostles") who represented the new movement. Of these, only Bill Hybels, Michael Fletcher and David Kim do not appear to have Pentecostal or charismatic backgrounds. Most of them—such as Billy Joe Daugherty, Roberts Liardon and William Kumuyi—are openly Pentecostal or charismatic. Others have been equally identified as part of the Pentecostal/charismatic renewal for years. One of these, the Redeemed Christian Church of God, led by Enoch Adeboye, states that it is "A Nigeria-based Pentecostal Holiness Ministry." Another, the Caananland Ministry led by David Oyedepo, describes itself as a Pentecostal-type church with links to the Faith

Movement in the United States. Clearly, most of the New Apostolic Churches identified by Wagner have their roots in classical Pentecostalism, and their distinctive features were pioneered by Pentecostals through the years. They were successful pastors long before the apostolic movement began.

In 1999, Wagner organized his followers into an umbrella grouping with the name "International Coalition of Apostles" with Wagner listed as the "presiding apostle." New apostles could join and pay $69 a month as membership dues. Wagner listed the many types of apostles who could be members. They included:

"Vertical Apostles," which included:
- "Ecclesiastical, Functional, Apostolic team members, and Congregational apostles"

"Horizontal Apostles," which included:
- "Convening, Ambassadorial, Mobilizing, and Territorial apostles"
- "Marketplace Apostles" (undefined) and
- "Calling Apostles," those who call Christians together in unity[6]

My Reactions to the New Apostolic Movement

From the outset, I was concerned about any movement that claims to restore apostolic offices that exercise ultimate and unchecked authority in churches. The potential for abuse is enormous. Throughout church history, attempts to restore apostle as an office in the church have often ended up in heresy or caused incredible pain. These attempts seemed similar to the Discipleship/Shepherding movement that had done so much damage to the charismatic movement.

When Peter Wagner wrote me a letter asking me to join his New Apostolic Movement, he said that he was now the "presiding apostle" of a new "international coalition of apostles." Further, he told me he believed I was a "calling apostle," whose gift was to call Christians together in unity.

I thought and prayed about his invitation for several weeks before answering him. If God was in this movement, I didn't want to be opposed to a genuine move of the Holy Spirit. Yet as much as I loved and respected the great work Wagner had done over the years, I couldn't bring myself to join the new organization. I didn't consider myself to be an apostle, and I wrote him that at $69 a month, "I could not afford to be an apostle." Although Wagner has listed me as a critic of the New Apostolic Reformation, we continue to be good friends. I still respect him highly as one of the seminal thinkers of the last several decades.

In 2005, in the General Conference of the Pentecostal Holiness Church, I warned the bishop and delegates about adopting apostolic language in the manual of the denomination. I predicted that we might see "short-term growth, but long-term confusion." Only time will tell if my prophecy is correct. In reaction, the denomination appointed a commission to study the apostolic movement and bring it back to the highest level of the denomination for approval or rejection.

After months of work with many meetings, we produced a document that has been acclaimed in the broader Church world. In it, we recognized four types of apostles in the Scriptures.

1. The Foremost Apostle—Jesus Christ
2. The Foundational Apostles—The Twelve
3. The Functional Apostles—Eight others in the New Testament (and which would include missionary apostles in all succeeding ages)
4. The False Apostles—who could appear in any age[7]

Further, we found that the term "office" had not continued to be used for those claiming to be apostles. Rather, the operative word was "ministry." In other words, it seems that the New Testament called for governing authority to be given to bishops and elders, while apostolic ministry continued as the church sent out missionaries as "sent ones," who carried out the continuing ministry of apostle. The main source of ruling authority of later apostles was derived from the fact that, as founders of new churches, they exercised the authority of founding fathers. However, after the death of the founding missionary of a church, that authority was transferred to bishops.

In 2004, in his book *Aftershock! How the Second Apostolic Age Is Changing the Church*, Wagner made grandiose claims about this new movement. He claimed that the charismatic movement was "a vision unfulfilled" and that the New Apostolic Renewal Movement had taken its place as the wave of the future. Obviously, I disagree with Wagner's claim because I know that the Pentecostal and charismatic movements around the world continue to grow by leaps and bounds. The organized historic Protestant denominations have declined only in Western Europe and North America. But in most Third World countries, Pentecostals still lead the way in church growth. And in most countries in Asia, Africa and Latin America, the mainline churches are still being transformed by the charismatic movement.[8]

In spite of my reservations, I believe that if not abused, the apostolic movement might still motivate many Spirit-filled leaders to do the ministry of missionary-apostles in bringing the Gospel to the millions of unreached peoples of the world who have never heard the name of Jesus.

If so, Amen. So be it!

12

Things I Never Expected to See in My Lifetime

Born as a depression baby in 1934, I lived through two-thirds of the "century of the Holy Spirit," allowing me to truly be an eyewitness to many events. Thankfully, God has also allowed me to live well into the twenty-first century.

During all these years, as I've shared in these pages, I've always taken an intense interest in all things religious. However, I've also followed the news of the political world with almost equal interest. As a teacher of both church history and American and world history, I followed major historical events not just for myself but for my students.

Even as a child I was curious about the history of my home state of Virginia, given that so many historical events happened near where I lived. I was especially interested in the Colonial, Revolutionary and Civil War periods. My major area of study in college and graduate school was American social and intellectual history. I also studied American, European and East Asian history for my Ph.D. studies at the University of Georgia.

People might assume that, having grown up Pentecostal in a preacher's home, my horizons were extremely limited. But this wasn't the case in my home. My father had a keen interest in national and international events. Newspaper articles and radio broadcasts were topics of conversation around the dinner table as we discussed current national and international events.

Later on, when I graduated from the University of Richmond, I was given the Vernon-Allport aptitude test. This "forced choice" exam indicated the test taker's major areas of interest. To the professor's amazement, I scored very high on both religion and politics. He said that I would probably be a good church politician.

In 2006, I was asked to be the graduation speaker at the Evangelical University in Sophia, the capital of Bulgaria. The university is made up of three Pentecostal seminaries and one fundamentalist evangelical school. I wanted to speak on the centennial of the Azusa Street Revival, but I was advised that the fundamentalists might not appreciate the topic. So, I spoke on "things I never expected to see in my lifetime." Because I was the first Pentecostal ever to give the commencement address, I made the Pentecostals very happy. But the fundamentalists were quite upset.

The following are the things I told them that I never expected to see in my lifetime, plus additional insights I've gleaned since then, as time and history march on.

In the Political World

I grew up as a child during World War II in eastern Virginia near Norfolk. Some of my early grammar school memories were of air raid drills, where we all had to file outside. We also had blackouts at night where all the lights in the city were turned off. The sounds of fighter planes overhead were frightening. In school, we also were told about the Axis powers—Germany, Italy and Japan. I recall seeing graphic photos of the war, as well as grisly and ghastly photos of the Nazi extermination camps in *Life* magazine. I also saw German prisoners of war who were housed in peanut warehouses in Suffolk. Locals laughed at their German speech.

People had great fear that America would be invaded by the Germans and Japanese. Indeed, American ships were sunk by German U-boats right off the coast, a few miles from where we lived. The power of Hitler and his seemingly invincible armies filled our hearts with dread. It seemed that the "thousand-year Reich" Hitler proclaimed could actually come to pass. Yet what seemed impossible became possible as the Americans fought bravely to win the war.

I remember playing in a Little League baseball game when the war ended in Europe and the local sirens blasted out the news. We all ran off the field and made our way to downtown Suffolk, where I saw a scene forever etched in my memory. The streets were full of cars with horns blaring while people danced in the streets. A few weeks later, after we had moved to nearby Hopewell, Virginia, the same scene took place on VJ day with the surrender of Japan.

Many people wondered if peace would reign for the rest of our lives. Of course, this was not to be. Just after the war ended, the Cold War began when Russia shot down an American airplane. Now a new reign of terror descended on the world. The Communists also seemed to be invincible as they took nation after nation in Europe and East Asia. When the Korean War began in 1950, I was certain that the Rapture of the Church was just around the corner. After that war ended in stalemate, the Vietnam War started just a few years later. Because I was in college, I wasn't drafted to serve in Vietnam, although I had fears of eventually dying in some Asian jungle. We worried that communism would continue to expand around the world, spreading atheism and socialism.

However, the time came when one impossible dream became a reality. In 1989, I was invited by William Kumuyi to join him in an evangelistic crusade in Moscow in the famous Izmailovo sports palace, which had been the weightlifting venue of the Moscow Olympics in 1980. Although Mikhail Gorbachev and the Communists were still in power, we preached to more than three thousand Russians each night. Hundreds of people were converted and healed. One day, I had the opportunity to speak to three hundred Pentecostal pastors in a special session on history. I was deeply moved as they spoke of years spent in prison for preaching the Gospel. I also preached in the First Pentecostal Church of Moscow, something I never dreamed could ever happen.

Then in 1990, the day came when the Berlin Wall fell, signaling the end of communism in Europe. I'll never forget this day either. Suddenly the spread of what seemed to be an implacable system set in concrete was gone. My mind went to Revelation 14:8 "Babylon is fallen, is fallen, that great city."

Another evil system that seemed unchangeable was the Jim Crow system of racial separation in the American South. This legal system had lasted for three centuries in my native Virginia, and I never thought I'd live to see the day when black people and white people would eat in the same restaurants, sleep in the same hotels, study in the same schools or worship in the same churches. With the racial attitudes that permeated the South when I was growing up, it seemed that this system could never change. Yet in 1954, the Supreme Court issued the *Brown vs. Board of Education* decision that in time changed everything. In those days, it was unthinkable that a black person could ever be elected president of the United States. Yet I lived to see the day in 2008 when Barack Hussein Obama was elected as president. Although I didn't share his political views, I was happy to see that the United States had come so far so fast to bring equality of opportunity to all its citizens. I also marvel that Regent University, where I served twelve years as dean of the School of Divinity, now counts African Americans as more than a third of its student body. This came not as a result of affirmative action, but because Regent welcomed all people as well as the Holy Spirit to its campus.

In a similar vein, I never expected the apartheid system of racial segregation to fall in South Africa. As a sophomore at Emmanuel College in 1955, I wrote a term paper on South Africa and its severe racial problems. I couldn't see any way of change short of bloodshed in the light of the implacable system of total separation in that land. In later years, I visited South Africa before the fall of the apartheid system. Although I saw Christians both supporting and resisting the system, I still feared that it would take a bloodbath to settle the issue. Yet the time came when the Babylon of apartheid fell in South Africa, with a peaceful transfer of power without the shedding of one drop of blood. To me, it was one of the greatest miracles in my lifetime to see Nelson Mandela peacefully elected as the president of the nation.

One of the most unexpected events in my lifetime was the rise of militant Islamic fundamentalism, which came to prominence with the Iranian hostage crises that occurred under President Jimmy Carter in 1979. We had always seen the Muslims in the Middle East as poor and peaceful nomads who could never threaten anyone, much less the modern nations of the West. But as Golda Maier once said, "Moses sent the children of Israel to the only piece of real estate in the Middle East that had no oil." Along with most Pentecostals, I was stunned when Israel became a nation in 1948. To us, it meant that the Second Coming of Christ was at the door. Of course, we believed that Israel would suddenly accept Jesus Christ as Savior and King some time during the tribulation period after the premillennial Rapture of the Church. Therefore, we were always strongly pro-Israel along with most of the American people.

On the fateful day of September 11, 2001, a documentary that I had helped to prepare was scheduled to appear on the MSNBC series *Captured*. It was titled, "Pentecostals Moving Millions." Sadly, the program didn't air on 9/11 because of the destruction of the twin towers of the World Trade Center in New York City by Islamic terrorists. Although the documentary was shown several times later, the tragedy in New York that knocked us off the air was ominous indeed.

I have come to believe that 9/11 was a new Pearl Harbor for the United States. In the long run, the threat of militant Islamic terrorism may be more dangerous and longer lasting than the threats of fascism and communism. Because Islamic terrorism is a politico-religious movement intent on conquering the world for Islam, it can count on fanatic extremists such as suicide bombers to continue the battle for generations to come. I also believe that the major hope for the Christian world would be a worldwide revival and awakening that would include the conversion of millions of Muslims to Christ. The major political hope would be for moderate elements in Muslim nations to gain political control of their governments and put an end to the radical terrorist organizations and their pernicious activities.

I recall seeing the early face of Islamic terrorism while teaching at Southwestern College in Oklahoma City in the mid-1970s. Hundreds of Muslims from Middle Eastern countries enrolled in the school, hoping to transfer to the University of Oklahoma to study petroleum technology. In spite of the fact that most of them could barely read, write or speak English, they were admitted, mainly for financial reasons. One day, we saw the distant future when we went to the chapel auditorium for a scheduled faculty meeting. To our surprise, the Muslim students had gathered there without permission from the college administrators to view a film. Some of us looked through the door and saw a film showing how to set up roadside bombs and how to sabotage cities and industries. Although we didn't realize the prophetic significance of the film, we were seeing a preview of what would happen in the first decade of the twenty-first century.

On the American scene, I never could have foreseen the rise of the "Christian Right" to political dominance in the 1980s and 1990s. The only time I voted Democratic was in the presidential election of 1976, when Jimmy Carter ran for president against Gerald Ford. When Carter ran for governor of Georgia in 1971, we invited him to speak in the chapel service at Emmanuel College in Franklin Springs, Georgia, where I taught American history and government. When I asked him to sit in on my government class, he came and taught for a full hour. In his talk, he gave a clear testimony of being a born-again Christian. I was impressed to vote for Carter. When I went to the courthouse in Carnesville to register to vote, I debated all the way whether I should register as a Republican or Democrat. When I arrived, they told me that I had no choice: all white people in Franklin County, Georgia, were Democrats whether they liked it or not. Still, I voted for Carter even though he was a Baptist and a Democrat.

In later years, the Christian Right came to prominence with the forceful activism of Jerry Falwell and his "Moral Majority," along with Pat Robertson and his "Christian Coalition." The elections of Ronald Reagan and George H. W. Bush to the White House were won with the overwhelming support of the evangelicals and Pentecostals who were pillars of the "Christian Right." With their strong support for right-to-life issues, for religious freedom around the world and for "faith based" government social programs, I felt that these presidents largely reflected the beliefs of most evangelicals and Pentecostals, who were mostly rock-ribbed conservatives.

In the Pentecostal World

Probably the most unexpected thing I observed in the Pentecostal world was the rapid rise of Pentecostal churches after World War II. Because the established Pentecostal denominations were so small and unpopular when I was growing up, I assumed that things would never change. When we drove by the large and beautiful high-steeple buildings of the Baptist, Methodist, Presbyterian and Catholic churches in town, it seemed that we were indeed small and unimportant.

Things changed after World War II. Pentecostals also began to build large, beautiful church buildings with money they'd saved during the war. In addition, more of us did well in school and some went on to become doctors, lawyers and schoolteachers. In our own church in Hopewell, attendance began to rise so much that every seat was taken for almost all services. Other pastors became curious about our growth and sometimes inquired about what we believed. As was true throughout the South, most factory managers and other employers highly prized Pentecostal workers because they didn't drink, smoke or lay out of work. They were generally hardworking, honest and sober. I later learned that in Chile, employers posted signs saying, "Help wanted. Only Pentecostals need apply."

In the early 1950s, our church in Hopewell made plans to build a new sanctuary that would seat seven hundred people. During the summer, I worked on the crew that carried mud, bricks and cinder blocks to the brick masons. I also painted the high outside windows. On the joyous day that the church was dedicated, almost five hundred people came from all over town. We were very proud. During the solemn ceremonies, we hoped that we wouldn't be embarrassed by someone shouting or falling out in the Spirit. What was happening in Hopewell was happening all over the nation. At this time in some cities, the largest church in town was the local Assemblies of God, Church of God or Pentecostal Holiness Church. Since my father regularly read all the Pentecostal denominational periodicals, I saw firsthand that the same kind of growth was occurring everywhere in the Pentecostal world.

This growth wasn't limited to the United States, as Pentecostalism began to grow astronomically throughout the world. I was later astonished to read David du Plessis's estimate that by 1945, there were more than twelve million Pentecostals in the world. While that number didn't seem possible to me at the time, the figure seemed more reasonable in later years. A large part of Pentecostal growth in America occurred among immigrant groups that poured into the country after the war. New York City was an early example of Pentecostal growth among the newly arrived masses from Puerto Rico. They soon honeycombed the city with storefront churches. The same was true for American blacks, who moved en masse from the South to northern cities. Harlem was soon filled with storefront Pentecostal churches of a bewildering variety. In later years, tens of thousands of Haitians, Indians, Latin Americans and many others began to populate the city.

In April 2001, a friend sent me an article from the *Wall Street Journal* titled "The Pentecostal City." When I saw this, I was sure that the city had to be Springfield, Missouri, or Cleveland, Tennessee, or Tulsa, Oklahoma—places known to be centers of Pentecostalism. To my surprise, the Pentecostal city in the article was New York City. The writer noted that more than 3,800 Pentecostal churches were listed in the New York City telephone directory. This didn't even include a huge number of small congregations that had no phones. The article also listed more than a hundred Pentecostal Bible schools and seminaries in the city. Another study in 2007 set the number of Pentecostal churches as 4,070. In addition to these churches, large numbers of Catholic charismatic prayer groups dotted the cities' ethnic communities. Prominent among these were Haitians, Hispanics and Koreans. What was happening wasn't unique to New York City, but was taking place in most major American urban areas.[1]

I also didn't expect to see the rise and success of the healing crusade ministries after World War II. A large part of the growth and popularity of Pentecostalism came as a result of the crusades of Oral Roberts in the United States and T. L. Osborn in many Third World countries. These mass crusades attracted multitudes of both the curious and the serious seekers for healing. Other healing evangelists such as William Branham, Thomas Wyatt and Jack Coe attracted huge crowds to their services. Thousands of those who attended these crusades later joined Pentecostal churches after the tents were taken down and the evangelists moved on to other cities.

The phenomenon of televangelists followed the healing ministries after 1953 when Oral Roberts put television cameras in his tent services to record his healing-line prayers. Suddenly, Pentecostals who had called televisions "hellivisions" and referred to rabbit-ear antennas as "devil's ears" were buying TVs by the thousands to watch Oral's crusades. In a way, Roberts "sanctified" television for Pentecostals. Following Oral were later televangelists that included Jimmy Swaggart, Jim Bakker, Kathryn Kuhlman, Kenneth Copeland and Joyce Meyer. Not long after came Christian TV networks led by Pat Robertson and his Christian Broadcasting Network (CBN) and Paul Crouch with his Trinity Broadcasting Network (TBN). Other preachers such as Bishop Sheen (Catholic), Robert Schuler (Reformed Church in America) and Charles Stanley (Southern Baptist Convention) were very popular. However the Pentecostals usually led in the ratings—and later caused more scandals than all the others combined.[2]

As far as the general public was concerned, interest in such Pentecostal distinctives as speaking in tongues and divine healing continued to grow into the twenty-first century. Not only did MSNBC carry a documentary on the growth of Pentecostalism, called "Pentecostals Moving Millions," the ABC network also asked me to help in producing a short documentary on speaking in tongues. I was told that the ABC staff was "fascinated" with the tongues phenomenon. I worked with religion editor Peggy Wehmeyer to produce a fifteen-minute story on *Primetime Live* with Diane Sawyer. In a very fair and objective manner, this piece showed the dynamics of tongues speaking in a megachurch in Tampa, Florida, led by Randy and Paula White. To me, this indicated that the attraction of Pentecostalism was destined to continue in the new century.

In the Charismatic World

I was indeed surprised when I heard of the mainline Protestant Neo-Pentecostals in 1960. While Pentecostalism had been largely ignored by most mainline denominations, the conservative Holiness and fundamentalist denominations had been the most outspoken critics of what they called "the tongues movement." The stories of Dennis Bennett, Brick Bradford, Larry Christenson, Howard Conatser and Tommy Tyson made a deep impression on me. Eventually I was to work closely with all of them in the great congresses of the 1980s and 1990s. To think of mainline Protestants speaking in tongues, praying for the sick and casting out demons all while staying in their mainline denominational churches was unimaginable. And yet, it was happening before our very eyes.

Perhaps the most unexpected "surprise of the Holy Spirit" was the news of the Catholic charismatic movement in 1967. When I first read about it, I was certain that the "Catholic Pentecostals," as they were first called, would soon be excommunicated from the Roman Catholic Church. So it was surprising to read the American bishops' report of 1969, which advised caution but urged allowing the movement to continue. I was even more surprised when I was called on to play a significant role in the development of Catholic Pentecostalism through my books, by speaking in major Catholic charismatic conferences and as I headed large ecumenical congresses where Catholics were always the largest single registered group. I never would have dreamed that I would be a close friend to Catholic bishops and even cardinals such as Joseph Suenens. To top it all, I never could have imagined joining with 1,500 Catholic charismatics in the Papal Retreat in Castel Gondolfo to meet Pope John Paul II in person and to hear him speak strongly in support of Catholic charismatics.

Over the years, I worked closely with such Catholic leaders as Kevin and Dorothy Ranaghan, Bert Ghezzi, Steve Clark, Bill Beatty, Tom Forrest, David Sklorenko and Nancy Kellar. Among the bishops I knew best were Joseph McKinney and Sam Jacobs. On my trips to Rome, I also got to know Peter and Marjorie Grace and Veronica O'Brien. In addition to being charismatics, they were also avid members of the Legion of Mary. Together with Cardinal Suenens, we worked to establish Pentecost Sunday as a major ecumenical celebration of the birthday of the Church. Suenens even came at my invitation to speak at a Pentecost celebration that I organized in Oklahoma City. Although we worked hard to make this dream a reality, the idea of a universal birthday party for all Christians never took root.

In the World of Megachurches

I've always been interested in church growth and the rise of "megachurches" in recent decades. In 1966, when I visited Chile for the first time, I spoke in the Jotabeche Pentecostal Methodist Church in Santiago. With forty thousand members, it was the largest Protestant congregation in the world at the time. I became a close friend of the pastor, Javier Vasquez, and his family. Vasquez also served as bishop of the denomination for many years.

I also became a good friend of David Yonggi Cho, pastor of the Yoido Full Gospel Church in Seoul, Korea. On several occasions, I've preached in his church of more than eight hundred thousand members. It is considered the largest local church in the history of Christianity. In these churches, as well as many others I have visited, the excitement was incredible as thousands of worshipers sang, danced and praised the Lord with crescendos of loud praise. I've called these huge congregations the "bell churches" because they all have little bells on the podium that are sounded when it's time to stop praying or rejoicing. I have sometimes jokingly called these bells "Spirit quenchers."

Many church growth experts agree that newer independent charismatic churches are the largest and fastest-growing churches in the United States and around the world. Some also see these churches as leaders in the "apostolic" movement as described by Peter Wagner. Many of them could be described as promoting the "prosperity gospel" as propounded by Oral Roberts, Kenneth Copeland and others.

For many years, the "ranker" versions of the prosperity gospel have been soundly condemned by many church leaders and particularly by professors in academia. Although I agree with most of these criticisms, in my travels to many countries and preaching in many of these large churches, I have come to see that they are fighting the same poverty and hopelessness that the liberal "social gospel" advocates crusade against. As I see it, the big difference is the means of overcoming poverty. These social gospel liberals believe that poverty will be overcome through government programs, socialism or communist revolution. On the other hand, the new Pentecostal and charismatic teachers believe that prosperity will come through hard work, the free market and the blessings of God. I've recently come to believe that this latter emphasis will ultimately result in "redemption and lift" of whole segments of the Christian population, as described by Donald McGavran of Fuller Theological Seminary.

In the Academic World

When I was growing up in the small town of Suffolk, Virginia, I never imagined that one day I'd serve as the dean of a school of divinity just 25 miles from my home, in a great university founded by a tongues-speaking Southern Baptist, Pat Robertson. Of course, the school is Regent University, which was founded in 1978 as an evangelical school with a distinctive charismatic flavor. When it opened, I somehow believed that I would teach there some day. I felt that this would be a great university under the brilliant leadership of Robertson.

But my path to Regent was preceded by teaching positions at Emmanuel College, my alma mater, and at Oklahoma City Southwestern College, also a church college where I served for a few months as interim president. After finishing twelve years as a general official of my denomination, I went to another school that I knew I'd probably serve at some time in the future, Oral Roberts University. Indeed, Oral Roberts had once offered to send me to Harvard, Yale or Princeton, and pay all my expenses if I'd return and teach at ORU. He wanted me to study theology, but my course was set. I couldn't imagine majoring in anything but history, and I'd already been awarded a full-ride scholarship to the University of Georgia to study American history. I've often wondered what would have happened if I'd accepted Oral's generous offer.

At Regent University, after I met with Robertson and explained that I'd never been a part of the discipleship/shepherding movement, I was called in the summer of 1994 by the faculty search committee and president Terry Lindvall to come to take up my responsibilities as dean. For the next twelve years, I led the School of Divinity in one of the most fulfilling periods of my life. In addition to tripling the student body, I led in creating the first Ph.D. online program in the world. This was done as a joint program with the School of Communication led by Dean Bill Brown with his assistant Bob Schihl. Our star professor was David Barrett, editor of the influential *World Christian Encyclopedia*.[3]

In the years to come, I also helped start a Doctor of Ministry (D.Min.) program and the first Ph.D. program in the world in a renewal-oriented university. With the hiring of such imminent scholars as Peter Grabe, Graham Twelftree, Stan Burgess and Amos Yong, the program was the first to be accredited by the Association of Theological Schools (ATS) as a nontraditional and nonresidential program. I never enjoyed a situation more wonderful anywhere else in my life. One of my pleasures was to become a golfing buddy with Pat Robertson. I found him to be as down to earth in private as he was brilliant in public. I vowed never to release his golf scores if he would never disclose mine—a true golfer's "gentlemen's agreement."[4]

Things I Expect to See in the Future

Although I'm a historian with a perspective typically geared toward the past, I've often been asked to predict what might happen in the future of the Pentecostal and charismatic renewal. This has meant abandoning the task of surveying the past and becoming a prophet as I look toward the future. Although I've never claimed the gift of predicting the future, I do believe scholarship demands that researchers share their insights in order to warn future generations not to make the same mistakes of the past.

As I look back over a lifetime working in my church, in the broader ecumenical world and in academia, I try to take a long view toward the future as I share what I think lies over the horizon. With that in mind, here are ten predictions that I'll be brave enough to make:

1. The Pentecostal and charismatic movements—in all their different forms—will grow to make up more than half of all the Christians in the world in the twenty-first

century. These movements already claimed more than 25 percent of all Christians in A.D. 2000. And with present growth rates, along with the shrinking of mainline churches, this seems to be a certainty.

2. The Assemblies of God will become the largest single Protestant church family in the world. With more than sixty million members in the world by 2010 and with very rapid growth rates, this church should surpass the Anglicans, the Baptists, the Methodists and the Lutherans in their worldwide members, followers and/or adherents.
3. Pentecostals will eventually claim half the population of Africa, and in the long run, will outgrow Muslims in the battle for control of the continent.
4. Classical Pentecostals and Roman Catholic charismatics will become the majority of all Latin American national populations before the end of the twenty-first century.
5. Africa will be the salvation of the Anglican Communion as their fast-growing national churches eventually take control of the Anglican world. The North American and British branches of the Anglican world will diminish in size to become negligible and less-influential parts of the church. The American Episcopal Church might actually be expelled from the Lambeth Conference of Bishops by the end of the century. This might serve as the salvation of this historic communion. The same could well happen in other Protestant denominations.
6. Through the mass healing crusades of Pentecostal evangelists such as Reinhard Bonnke and Benny Hinn, Pentecostal and charismatic Christianity will become more than 10 percent of the population of India.
7. China will have the largest Christian population in the world by the end of the twenty-first century. Pentecostal

and charismatic churches will make up the vast majority of these new Christians. Along with this revival will come the end of Communist rule in China and the institution of true democracy.

8. Because of very high birth rates, the number of Muslims will increase in most Western nations, including Britain, Germany, France and the United States. The world population of Muslims will climb during the century because many Christians practicing birth control will have smaller families, and because most Western nations have massive abortion rates. The only possibility for change in this trend would be a mighty revival of signs and wonders that will convert hundreds of millions of Muslims to Christianity.
9. In time, as the Pentecostal and charismatic movements continue to grow, more than half of the heads of state in the world will be Pentecostals or charismatics. Demographic growth has always been followed by political influence and power.
10. The future of Christian affairs will be more and more in the hands of the massively growing Pentecostal churches and a Roman Catholic Church that has been renewed and energized by the charismatic renewal.

Dreams That Seemed Impossible

Because many things that once seemed impossible have happened in my lifetime, I often hum the words of an old popular song that I heard in my youth: "Dreams that seemed impossible all at last have come true, now I see."

As I reflect on what I've written in these pages, many of the darkest clouds that seemed so threatening and even lethal have passed over to be forgotten and cast onto the scrapheap of history. These storm clouds included fascism, communism, racial segregation in America and apartheid in South Africa. I'm convinced that in the future, the threat of Islamic terrorism will join the others on the same scrapheap.

Years ago, I had an experience that taught me never to give in to what seems to be an impossible situation. On a trip to Chile, where I was to preach in the largest church in the world at the time, I caught an early afternoon flight from Atlanta to Miami. In Miami, I would catch a long overnight flight to Santiago, where I knew that Bishop Vasquez and hundreds of his members would welcome me at the airport.

As I usually do when traveling, once I settled in my seat, I decided to check my travel documents. When I looked at my passport, I was stunned to see that it had expired three months earlier. A cold sweat broke out on my brow. What should I do? Should I go back home and phone the pastor to say that I wouldn't be able to come?

Something inside of me rebelled at backing out of this seemingly impossible situation. I prayed desperately, and I received this answer: *Just go as far as you can until someone turns you back*. I believed this message was from the Lord, so I decided to do just that.

When I got to the check-in counter in Miami, I showed my passport to the ticket agent. He looked at it, and motioned for me to enter. I didn't dare point out that my passport had expired. I thought that maybe he couldn't read.

Then, when I went through U.S. customs, I was again waved through, no questions asked. I was cleared to fly on the long trip to Santiago.

On the plane, I spent a sleepless night wondering what would happen when the Chilean customs agent saw my passport. But when I got to the customs desk, the agent looked at my passport for a long time, then stamped it and waved me on.

Because I was now legally inside the country, I asked the agent why he didn't see that my passport had expired. He answered, "Yes, of course I saw it. But didn't you know that three months ago, the U.S. Congress passed a law extending all American passports for another three years?" Wow!

Apparently, I was the only one on the trip who didn't know about the new extension. I gave one great "Hallelujah" as I walked down the concourse to greet my Chilean friends.

In the end, what seemed to be an impossible situation turned out to be nothing at all! I learned a lifelong lesson from this experience: "Go as far as you can until someone turns you back."

And this testimony is what I now offer to the multitudes of Christians in the Pentecostal and charismatic movements of the world. Keep on going ahead, because nothing or no one can turn you back as long as you move forward in the Spirit and do not stray from the clear teachings of Scripture.

After spending my life as an eyewitness to both the successes and failures of this mighty spiritual move of God in the twentieth and twenty-first centuries, I am more encouraged now than at any other time in my life. The future is limitless as long as we keep the Pentecostal fires burning, the gifts of the Spirit in operation and the evangelization of the world as our ultimate goal. And all of this will be done:

> "Not by might nor by power, but by My Spirit," says the Lord of hosts.
>
> Zechariah 4:6

Notes

Chapter One A Child of Azusa Street

1 Much of my family history can be found in my book: Vinson Synan, *The Synans of Virginia: The Story of an Irish Family in America* (Fairfax, Va.: Xulon Press, 2003). Also important was my father's diary from 1934 to 1983.

2. See Frank Bartleman, *How "Pentecost" Came to Los Angeles* (N.P., 1925). The best source of these quotations is: Mel Robeck, *The Azusa Street Mission and Revival* (Nashville: Thomas Nelson, 2006).

3. I covered this part of the story in detail in my book: Vinson Synan, *The Holiness Pentecostal Tradition* (Grand Rapids: Eerdmans, 1971, 1997).

4. See Lindsay Synan, *Running the Race* (Franklin Springs, Ga.: Advocate Press, 1985).

Chapter Two The Latter Rain and Healing Revivals

1. I heard Katie Campbell make this statement many times. She might have borrowed it from Aimee Semple McPherson.

2. A very good account of this revival is: Richard Riss, *Latter Rain Movement of 1948* (Mississauga, Ontario: Honeycomb Visual Productions, 1987). Also see William Faupel, *The Everlasting Gospel* (Sheffield, UK: Academic Press, 1996).

3. I heard T. A. Melton make this statement with my own ears.

4. The best biography of Oral Roberts is: David Harrell, *Oral Roberts: An American Life* (Bloomington, Ind.: Indiana University Press, 1985).

5. Most of this period is covered in my book: Vinson Synan, *The Old Time Power: A History of the Pentecostal Holiness Church* (Franklin Springs, Ga.: Advocate Press, 1973, 1997).

6. Vinson Synan, *Under His Banner: A History of the Full Gospel Business Men's Fellowship International* (Costa Mesa, Calif.: Gift Publications, 1992).

7. For the story of Emmanuel College, see my book: Vinson Synan, *Emmanuel College: The First Fifty Years* (Washington, D.C.: North Washington Press, 1968).

8. *Time,* June 21, 1971, 58.

9. The Chilean story can be found in my book: Vinson Synan, *Century of the Holy Spirit: 100 Years of Pentecostal and Charismatic Renewal* (Nashville: Thomas Nelson, 2001), 309–11.

10. The story of the Society for Pentecostal Studies can be found in: William Faupel, *The Society for Pentecostal Studies: Commemorating Thirty Years of Annual Meetings* (Lexington, Ky., 2001).

Chapter Three Protestant Neo-Pentecostals

1. The story of the Protestant renewal can be found in my book: Vinson Synan, *The Twentieth Century Pentecostal Explosion* (Lake Mary, Fla.: Creation House, 1987).

2. See Rodman Williams, *A Theological Pilgrimage*, http://www.jrodmanwilliams.net/.

Chapter Four Catholic Charismatics

1. Excellent histories of the Protestant and Catholic charismatic movements can be found in Kilian McDonnell, *The Charismatic Movement in the Churches* (New York: Seabury Press, 1976).

2. Kilian McDonnell, *Catholic Pentecostalism: Problems in Evaluation* (Pecos, N.Mex.: Dove Publications, 1970).

3. See Kevin and Dorothy Ranaghan, *Catholic Pentecostals* (Paramus, N.J.: Paulist Press, 1969). In the early days, they were known as Catholic Pentecostals rather than Catholic charismatics.

4. Edward O'Connor, *The Pentecostal Movement in the Catholic Church* (Notre Dame: Ave Maria Press, 1971).

5. Bob Slosser and David du Plessis, *A Man Called Mr. Pentecost* (Plainfield, N.J.: Logos International, 1977).

6. See Synan, *The Old Time Power*, 280–83.

Chapter Five Charismatic Concerns and Controversies

1. This story is told best in: David Moore, *The Shepherding Movement: Controversy and Charismatic Ecclesiology* (London: T & T Clark International, 2003).

2. Ibid.

3. Vinson Synan, *A Seminary to Change the World: Regent University School of Divinity at 25 Years* (Virginia Beach, Va.: Regent University, 2007), 11–12.

4. Ralph Martin, "God is Restoring His People," *New Covenant*, Sept. 1974, 3–6. Also see: Ralph Martin, *Fire on the Earth* (Ann Arbor: Servant Books, 1975).

5. The story of the conference is told in: David Manuel, *Like a Mighty River* (Orleans, Mass.: Rock Harbor Press, 1977).

6. See Manuel, *Like a Mighty River*, 9–26. The words were transcribed from the documentary film of the conference.

7. Manuel, *Like a Mighty River*, 196–97.

8. This is found in: Vinson Synan, *In the Latter Days: The Outpouring of the Holy Spirit in the Twentieth Century* (Ann Arbor: Servant Publications, 1984), 127–28. Also see Manuel, *Like a Mighty River*, 195.

Chapter Six New Orleans

1. Most of the details of the Glencoe meetings are given in: David Moore, *The Shepherding Movement.*

2. These quotations are transcribed from the conference documentary film *Blow the Trumpet in Zion.*

3. See Julia Duin, "The Holy Spirit and World Evangelization," *Christianity Today,* September 4, 1987, 44–45. Also see Steven Lawson, "The Big Charismatic Get-Together," *Charisma,* September 1987, 56–57.

Chapter Seven The Prosperity Gospel

1. Hank Hanegraaff, *Christianity in Crisis* (Eugene, Ore.: Harvest House Publishers, 1993).

2. Russell Conwell, *Acres of Diamonds* (New York, London: Harper & Brothers, 1915). Andrew Carnegie, *The Gospel of Wealth* (Cambridge, Mass.: Belknap Press of Harvard University Press, 1962).

3. Donald McGavran, *The Bridges of God* (New York: Friendship Press, 1955); Donald McGavran, *Understanding Church Growth* (Grand Rapids: Eerdmans, 1970).

4. Napoleon Hill, *Think and Grow Rich* (New York: Fawcett Crest, 1960).

5. Oral Roberts, *The Miracle of Seed Faith* (Old Tappan, N.J.: Revell, 1970). Also see Oral Roberts, *Expect a Miracle: My life and Ministry; An Autobiography* (Nashville: Thomas Nelson, 1995).

6. David Yonggi Cho, *The Fourth Dimension* (Plainfield, N.J.: Logos International, 1979).

Chapter Eight The Third Wave

1. Peter Wagner, *Your Spiritual Gifts Can Help Your Church Grow* (Glendale, Calif.: Regal Books, 1979).

2. Peter Wagner, *On the Crest of the Wave: Becoming a World Christian* (Ventura, Calif.: Regal Books, 1983).

3. Stan Burgess, et.al. *International Dictionary of Pentecostal Charismatic Movements* (Grand Rapids: Zondervan, 2002), 1141.

4. Dennis Bennett, "The Old Paths," *Morning Watch,* Spring 1989.

5. Vinson Synan and Ralph Rath, *Launching the Decade of Evangelism* (South Bend: NARSC, 1990), 139–44.

6. Vinson Synan, *The Spirit Said "Grow"* (Monrovia, Calif.: MARC, 1992).

7. David Barrett, George T. Kurian and Todd M. Johnson, *World Christian Encyclopedia: A Comparative Survey of Churches and Religions in the Modern World* (New York: Oxford University Press, 2001).

Chapter Nine Racial Reconciliation

1. Brewster and his church were locally famous and influential, not only for the music and preaching, but for holding racially integrated services prior to the civil rights movement.

2. See Cindy Hazen and Mike Freeman, *Memphis Elvis-Style* (Memphis: John F. Blair, 1997), one of the books documenting the influence of East Trigg Baptist on the music style of Elvis Presley.

3. Personal interview with the author.

4. Synan, *Holiness Pentecostal Tradition*, 167–86.

5. Bartleman, *How "Pentecost" Came to Los Angeles*, 54.

6. Synan, *Holiness Pentecostal Tradition*, 211.

7. These events are described in: Manuel, *Like a Mighty River*, 147.

8. Most of this information on the Memphis Miracle comes from my own records and memory. A short treatment is given in my book: Synan, *Holiness Pentecostal Tradition,* 185. Also see, "Pentecostals Experience a Miracle in Memphis," *Memphis Commercial Appeal,* October 20, 1994; Barbara Reynolds, "Oregon Voters Can Learn from the Memphis Miracle," *USA Today*, October 25, 1994.

9. Much of this information comes from transcriptions of the conference documentary videos.

10. This prophecy is taken from the documentary video of the conference.

11. This can be found in *Reconciliation Journal,* 1998 summer edition, 17; also see Vinson Synan, ed., *Pentecostal Partners: A Reconciliation Strategy for 21st Century Ministry* (Memphis: privately printed, 1994).

Chapter Ten Toronto, Brownsville and Lakeland Revivals

1. For accounts of great awakenings, see Earl Cairns, *An Endless Line of Splendor* (Grand Rapids: Zondervan, 1988).

2. For eyewitness accounts of the Cane Ridge Camp Meeting, see *Barton Stone: A Spiritual Biography* (St. Louis, Mo.: Chalice Press, 2000). A great pictorial account of Cane Ridge can be found in "Camp Meetings and Circuit Riders," *Christian History* (Issue 45).

3. Timothy Smith, *Revivalism and Social Reform: American Protestantism on the Eve of the Civil War* (New York: Abingdon Press, 1957).

4. See "The Rise of Pentecostalism," *Christian History* (Issue 58).

5. See Riss, *Latter Rain Movement of 1948.*

6. Margaret Paloma, *Main Street Mystics* (Walnut Creek, Calif.: AltaMira Press, 2003).

7. See John Arnott, *The Father's Blessing* (Orlando: Creation House, 1995); Guy Chevreau, *Catch the Fire: The Toronto Blessing* (Toronto: Harper Collins, 1995).

8. Marcia Ford, *Charisma Reports: The Brownsville Revival* (Orlando: Creation House, 1997).

Chapter Eleven The New Apostolic Reformation Movement

1. See the *Didache* (11:3).

2. David Dorries, "Edward Irving and the Standing Sign" in Gary McGee, *Initial Evidence* (Peabody, Mass.: Hendrickson Publishers, 1991).

3. Rodney Stark, *The Rise of Mormonism* (New York: Columbia University Press, 2005).

4. David Cannistraci, *Apostles and the Emerging Apostolic Movement* (Ventura, Calif.: Renew Books, 1996).

5. Peter Wagner, *The New Apostolic Churches* (Ventura, Calif.: Regal Press, 1998), 13–25.

6. http://www.apostlesnet.net/prospectus.htm.

7. http://gso.iphc.org/apostles.html.

8. Peter Wagner, *Aftershock! How the Second Apostolic Age Is Changing the Church* (Ventura, Calif.: Regal Books, 2004).

Chapter Twelve Things I Never Expected to See in My Lifetime

1. Tony Carnes, "Houses of Worship: The Pentecostal City," *The Wall Street Journal,* April 13, 2001.

2. David Edwin Harrell, *All Things Are Possible: The Healing and Charismatic Revivals in Modern America* (Bloomington, Ind.: Indiana University Press, 1975).

3. See Synan, *A Seminary to Change the World.*

4. Pat Robertson, *Shout It from the Housetops* (Plainfield, N.J.: Logos International, 1972).

Bibliography

Anderson, Robert Mapes. *Vision of the Disinherited: The Making of American Pentecostalism*. New York: Oxford University Press, 1979.

Arnott, John. *The Father's Blessing*. Orlando, Fla.: Creation House, 1995.

Barrett, David, George T. Kurian, and Todd M. Johnson. *World Christian Encyclopedia: A Comparative Survey of Churches and Religions in the Modern World*. New York: Oxford University Press, 2001.

Bartleman, Frank. *How "Pentecost" Came to Los Angeles*. N.P., 1925.

Bennett, Dennis. "The Old Paths," *Morning Watch* (Spring 1989).

Blumhofer, Edith W. *The Assemblies of God: A Popular History*. Springfield, Mo.: Gospel Publishing House, 1985, 1989, two volumes.

Breckenridge, James F. *The Theological Self-Understanding of the Catholic Charismatic Movement*. Washington: University Press of America, 1980.

Bredesen, Harald. *Yes, Lord*. Plainfield, N.J.: Logos International, 1972.

Buchanan, Colin. *The Charismatic Movement in the Church of England*. London: CIO Publishing, 1981.

Burgess, Stan, et. al. *International Dictionary of Pentecostal Charismatic Movements*. Grand Rapids: Zondervan, 2002.

Cairns, Earl. *An Endless Line of Splendor*. Grand Rapids: Zondervan, 1988.

Cannistraci, David. *Apostles and the Emerging Apostolic Movement*. Ventura, Calif.: Renew Books, 1996.

Carnegie, Andrew. *The Gospel of Wealth*. Cambridge, Mass.: Belknap Press of Harvard University Press, 1962.

Carnes, Tony. "Houses of Worship: The Pentecostal City," *The Wall Street Journal* (April 13, 2001).

Cho, David Yonggi. *The Fourth Dimension*. Plainfield, N.J.: Logos International, 1979.

Chevreau, Guy. *Catch the Fire: The Toronto Blessing*. Toronto: Harper Collins, 1995, 1994.

Christenson, Larry. *The Charismatic Renewal Among Lutherans: A Pastoral and Theological Perspective*. Minneapolis: Lutheran Charismatic Renewal Services, 1976.

Christian History (Issue 45). "Camp Meetings and Circuit Riders."

Christian History (Issue 58). "The Rise of Pentecostalism."

Conwell, Russell. *Acres of Diamonds*. New York, London: Harper & Brothers, 1915.

Cox, Harvey. *Fire from Heaven*. Reading, Mass.: Addison-Wesley, 1995.

Culpetter, Robert H. *Evaluating the Charismatic Movement: A Theological and Biblical Appraisal*. Valley Forge, Pa.: Judson Press, 1977.

Damboriena, Prudencio. *Tongues as of Fire: Pentecostalism in Contemporary Christianity*. Washington: Corpus Books, 1969.

Derstine, Gerald. *Following the Fire*. Plainfield, N.J.: Logos International, 1980.

Dollar, George W. *The New Testament, The New Pentecostalism*. Minneapolis: Central Baptist Theological Seminary, 1978.

Dorries, David. "Edward Irving and the Standing Sign" in Gary McGee, *Initial Evidence*. Peabody, Mass.: Hendrickson Publishers, 1991.

Duin, Julia "The Holy Spirit and World Evangelization," *Christianity Today* (September 4, 1987), 44–45.

du Plessis, David J. *The Spirit Bade Me Go*. Plainfield, N.J.: Logos International, 1970.

Durasoff, Steve. *Bright Wind of the Spirit*. Plainfield, N.J.: Logos International, 1972.

Faupel, William. *The Everlasting Gospel*. Sheffield, UK: Academic Press, 1996.

———. *The Society for Pentecostal Studies: Commemorating Thirty Years of Annual Meetings*. Lexington, Ky., 2001.

Ford, J. Massyngberde. *Which Way for Catholic Pentecostals?* New York: Harper and Row, 1976.

Ford, Marcia. *Charisma Reports: The Brownsville Revival*. Orlando, Fla.: Creation House, 1997.

Fullam, Everett L. *Riding the Wind: Your Life in the Holy Spirit*. Altamonte Springs, Fla.: Creation House, 1986.

Gelpi, Donald L. *Pentecostalism: A Theological Viewpoint*. New York: Paulist Press, 1971.

Gunstone, John. *Pentecostal Anglicans.* London: Hodder & Stoughton, 1982.

Hanegraaff, Hank. *Christianity in Crisis.* Eugene, Ore.: Harvest House Publishers, 1993.

Harper, Michael. *As at the Beginning: The Twentieth Century Pentecostal Revival.* Plainfield, N.J.: Logos International, 1965.

Harrell, David Edwin. *All Things Are Possible: The Healing and Charismatic Revivals in Modern America.* Bloomington, Ind.: Indiana University Press, 1975.

———. *Oral Roberts: An American Life.* Bloomington, Ind.: Indiana University Press, 1985.

Hayford, Jack. *The Beauty of Spiritual Language: My Journey Toward the Heart of God.* Dallas: Word Publishing, 1992.

Hill, Napoleon. *Think and Grow Rich.* New York: Fawcett Crest, 1960.

Hollenweger, Walter. *The Pentecostals.* Peabody, Mass.: Hendrickson Publishers, 1988; first published in 1872.

Hummell, Charles G. *Fire in the Fireplace: Contemporary Charismatic Renewal.* Downers Grove, Ill.: InterVarsity Press, 1978.

Hunter, Harold. *Reconciliation Journal,* Summer 1998, 17.

Jorstad, Erling. *Bold in the Spirit: Lutheran Charismatic Renewal in America Today.* Minneapolis: Augsburg Publishing House, 1974.

Kelsey, Morton T. *Healing and Christianity in Ancient Thought and Modern Times.* New York: Harper and Row, 1976.

Kendrick, Klaude. *The Promise Fulfilled: A History of the American Pentecostal Movement.* Springfield, Mo.: Gospel Publishing House, 1961.

Laurentin, Rene. *Catholic Pentecostalism.* Garden City, N.J.: Doubleday, 1977.

Lawson, Steven. "The Big Charismatic Get-Together." *Charisma,* September 1987, 56–57.

Lindberg, Carter. *The Third Reformation? Charismatic Movements and the Lutheran Tradition.* Macon, Ga.: Mercer University Press, 1983.

MacArthur, John F., Jr., *The Charismatics: A Doctrinal Perspective.* Grand Rapids: Zondervan, 1978.

MacNutt, Francis. *Healing.* Notre Dame: Ave Maria, 1974.

Manuel, David. *Like a Mighty River.* Orleans, Mass.: Rock Harbor Press, 1977.

Martin, David. *Tongues of Fire: The Explosion of Protestantism in Latin America.* Cambridge, Mass.: Basil Blackwood, 1990.

Martin, Ralph. *Fire on the Earth.* Ann Arbor: Servant Books, 1975.

McConnell, D. R. *A Different Gospel.* Peabody, Mass.: Hendrickson Publishers, 1988.

McDonnell, Kilian. *Catholic Pentecostalism: Problems in Evaluation.* Pecos, N.Mex.: Dove Publications, 1970.

———. *Charismatic Movement and the Churches.* New York: Seabury Press, 1976.

McDonnell, Kilian, and George Montague. *Christian Initiation and Baptism in the Holy Spirit: Evidence from the First Eight Centuries.* Collegeville, Minn.: Liturgical Press, 1991.

McGavran, Donald. *The Bridges of God.* New York: Friendship Press, 1955.

———. *Understanding Church Growth.* Grand Rapids: Eerdmans, 1970.

McGee, Gary B., ed. *Initial Evidence: Historical and Biblical Perspectives on the Pentecostal Doctrine of Spirit Baptism.* Peabody, Mass.: Hendrickson Publishers, 1991.

Menzies, William. *Anointed to Serve: The Story of the Assemblies of God.* Springfield, Mo.: Gospel Publishing House, 1971.

Moore, David. *The Shepherding Movement: Controversy and Charismatic Ecclesiology.* London: T & T Clark International, 2003.

O'Connor, Edward D. *The Pentecostal Movement in the Catholic Church.* Notre Dame: Ave Maria Press, 1971.

Orr, James Edwin. *The Flaming Tongue: The Impact of the Twentieth Century Revivals.* Chicago: Moody Press, 1973.

Paloma, Margaret. *Main Street Mystics.* Walnut Creek, Calif.: AltaMira Press, 2003.

Ranaghan, Kevin and Dorothy. *Catholic Pentecostals.* Paramus, N.J.: Paulist Press, 1969.

Report of the Special Committee on the Work of the Holy Spirit. New York: PCUSA, Office of the General Assembly, 1970.

Reynolds, Barbara. "Oregon Voters Can Learn from the Memphis Miracle." *USA Today*, October 25, 1994, 11A.

Riss, Richard. *Latter Rain Movement of 1948.* Mississauga, Ontario: Honeycomb Visual Productions, 1987.

Robeck, Cecil M., Jr. *The Azusa Street Mission and Revival.* Nashville: Thomas Nelson, 2006.

———, ed. *Charismatic Experiences in History.* Peabody, Mass.: Hendrickson Publishers, 1985.

Roberts, Oral. *Expect a Miracle: My Life and Ministry.* Nashville: Thomas Nelson, 1985.

———. *The Miracle of Seed Faith.* Old Tappan, N.J.: Revell, 1970.

Robertson, Pat. *Shout It from the Housetops.* Plainfield, N.J.: Logos International, 1972.

Ruthven, Jon. *On the Cessation of the Charismata.* Sheffield, UK: Sheffield Academic Press, 1993.

Shakarian, Demos. *The Happiest People on Earth*. Old Tappan, N.J.: Chosen Books, 1975.

Sherrill, John. *They Speak with Other Tongues*. New York: McGraw and Hill, 1964.

Slosser, Bob, and David du Plessis. *A Man Called Mr. Pentecost*. Plainfield, N.J.: Logos International, 1977.

Smith, Timothy. *Revivalism and Social Reform: American Protestantism on the Eve of the Civil War*. New York: Abingdon Press, 1957.

Spittler, Russell. *Perspectives on the New Pentecostalism*. Grand Rapids: Baker Book House, 1976.

Stark, Rodney. *The Rise of Mormonism*. New York: Columbia University Press, 2005.

Stoll, David. *Is Latin America Turning Protestant?* Berkeley, Calif.: University of California Press, 1990.

Stone, Barton. *A Spiritual Biography*. St. Louis, Mo.: Chalice Press, 2000).

Suenens, Leon Joseph, Cardinal. *A New Pentecost?* New York: Seabury Press, 1974.

Synan, Lindsay C. *Running the Race*. Franklin Springs, Ga.: Advocate Press, 1985.

Synan, Vinson, ed. *Aspects of Pentecostal Charismatic Origins*. Plainfield, N.J.: Logos International, 1975.

———. *Century of the Holy Spirit*. Nashville: Thomas Nelson, 2001.

———. *Charismatic Bridges*. Ann Arbor: Word of Life, 1974.

———. *Emmanuel College: The First Fifty Years*. Washington, D.C.: North Washington Press, 1968.

———. *The Holiness Pentecostal Tradition*. Grand Rapids: Eerdmans, 1971, 1997.

———. *In the Latter Days: The Outpouring of the Holy Spirit in the Twentieth Century*. Ann Arbor: Servant Books, 1984.

———. *A Seminary to Change the World: Regent University School of Divinity at 25 Years*. Virginia Beach, Va.: Regent University, 2007.

———. *The Spirit Said "Grow."* Monrovia, Calif.: MARC, 1992.

———. *The Synans of Virginia: The Story of an Irish Family in America*. Fairfax, Va.: Xulon Press, 2003.

———. *Under His Banner: History of Full Gospel Business Men's Fellowship International*. Costa Mesa, Calif.: Gift Publications, 1992.

Synan, Vinson, and Ralph Rath. *Launching the Decade of Evangelization*. South Bend, Ind.: North American Renewal Service Committee, 1990.

Wacker, Grant. *Heaven Below, Early Pentecostals and American Culture*. Cambridge, Mass.: Harvard University Press, 2001.

Wagner, C. Peter. *Aftershock! How the Second Apostolic Age Is Changing the Church*. Ventura, Calif.: Regal Books, 2004.

———. *How to Have a Healing Ministry Without Making Your Church Sick*. Ventura, Calif.: Regal Books, 1988.

———. *The New Apostolic Churches.* Ventura, Calif.: Regal Books, 1998.

———. *On the Crest of the Wave: Becoming a World Christian*. Ventura, Calif.: Regal Books, 1983.

———. *Your Spiritual Gifts Can Help Your Church Grow.* Glendale, Calif.: Regal Books, 1979.

Warner, Wayne ed. *Touched by the Fire.* Plainfield, N.J.: Logos International, 1978.

Williams, J. Rodman. *Renewal Theology, Vols. 1–3*. Grand Rapids: Zondervan, 1988.

———. *A Theological Pilgrimage.* http://www.jrodmanwilliams.net.

Wimber, John. *Power Healing.* San Francisco: Harper and Row, 1987.

Index

700 Club, 82, 107, 160

Acres of Diamonds (Conwell), 120
AD 2000 Together, 134
Adeboye, Enoch, 115, 123, 182
Africa, 123, 138, 203
Aldersgate charismatic group, 90
altar calls, 25, 31, 47, 110, 164, 165–66
American Episcopal Church, 203
American Freedom and Catholic Power (Blanchard), 64
Amos, Barbara, 153
Anacondia, Carlos, 164
Anaheim Vineyard Church, 130, 136, 137–38
Anderson, Reuben, 148
Anthony, Ole, 115
apartheid, 191
apostles, 184–85
  bishops as successors of, 173
  definition of, 172–73
  fourfold offices of, 175
  Irvingite apostles, 174–77
  Mormon apostles, 177–79
  Pentecostal apostles, 179–81
  view of apostles by the established church, 173–74
  See also New Apostolic Reformation
Apostles and the Emerging Apostolic Movement (Cannistraci), 181
Apostolic Faith movement, 179–80
Aquinas, Thomas, 118
Argue, A. H., 23
Arnott, Carol, 158, 162
Arnott, John, 158, 161–62
Assemblies of God, 24, 33, 34, 36, 38, 77, 145, 180, 203. *See also* Brownsville Revival
Association of Vineyard Churches, 129
Ault, Steve, 165
Azusa Street Pilgrims, 23
Azusa Street Revival, 20, 21–22, 145, 179
  as the Fourth Great Awakening, 157
  legacy of, 22–24
  personal experience of Azusa-type of revival, 24–29
  and the whole body of Christ, 29–30

Bakker, Jim, 197
baptism. *See* Holy Spirit, the, baptism in; rebaptizing, of charismatics
Baptism in the Holy Spirit as an Ecumenical Problem (McDonnell), 66
Barratt, Thomas Ball, 23, 180
Barrett, David, 138, 201
Bartleman, Frank, 145
Basham, Don, 78, 79
Baxter, Ern, 78
Beacham, Paul F., 39
Beale, Myrtle, 35
Beatty, Bill, 68, 99, 101, 103, 199
Bennett, Dennis, 53–54, 58, 61, 78, 80, 82, 83, 91, 110–11, 128, 134–35, 135–36, 198
Bennett, Rita, 111
Bentley, Todd, 167–69
Berg, Daniel, 23
Bethesda Missionary Temple (Detroit), 35
Beverly Hills Baptist Church, 59–60
Bevis, Jim, 99
Bhengu, Nicolas, 40–41
Bittlinger, Arnold, 63, 72
Bixler, Russ, 60
Black Pentecostal Holiness Church, 142
Blake, Charles, 148, 150, 152
Blanchard, John, 64
Bonnke, Reinhard, 104–5, 110, 114, 123, 203
Boone, Pat, 78
Bouyer, Louis, 70
Bradford, Brick, 58, 86, 91, 97, 99, 198
Bradshaw, Charles, 74
Branham, William, 38, 196
Braxton, Lee, 39

Bredesen, Harald, 83
Bridges of God, The (McGavran), 120
Brown, Bill, 201
Brown, Jim, 54
Brown, Michael, 165
Brown, Rodney Howard, 158
Brown vs. Board of Education (1954), 191
Brownsville Revival (Brownsville Assemblies of God), 163–66, 169
Buckingham, Jamie, 83, 84, 105, 109
Burgess, Stan, 202
Burnett, Bill, 92
Bush, George H. W., 194

Caananland Ministry, 182–83
Calvary Pentecostal Camp Meeting, 36–37
Campbell, Joseph, Jr., 26
Campbell, Katie, 32, 207n1
Campbell, Mary, 175
Cannistraci, David, 181
Carnegie, Andrew, 119, 120
Carter, Jimmy, 191, 193
Cashwell, Gaston Barnabas, 20, 23, 180
Catholic Apostolic Church, 175, 176–77
Catholic Charismatic Conference, 63
Chappell, Paul, 39
charismata, 127
Charismatic Bridges (Vinson Synan), 85
Charismatic Concerns Committee, 84–85, 97
charismatic renewal, three streams of, 86–90, 91, 127, 157
Charismatic Renewal Services (CRS), 86, 87, 98, 107
Chile, Pentecostal Methodists of, 47–48
China, 202–3
Cho, David Yonggi, 50, 101, 102, 114, 123, 199
Christenson, Larry, 58, 59, 79, 81, 83, 84, 85, 86, 87, 92, 93, 97, 99, 147, 198
Christian Apostolic Church, 175
Christian Initiation and the Baptism in the Holy Spirit (Montague and McDonnell), 128
Christian Right, rise of, 193–94
Church of God, 29, 36, 38, 47, 90, 144, 145, 147, 180, 195
Church of God Evangel, 49
Clark, Gary, 59, 85, 99
Clark, Randy, 158
Clark, Steve, 67, 199
Clemmons, Ithiel, 86, 101, 147, 148, 153
Coe, Jack, 196
Collins, David, 60
Collins, Ginny, 60
communism, 189–90
Conatser, Howard, 59, 198
Conn, Charles, 49
Conwell, Russell, 119–20
Copeland, Kenneth, 110, 112, 114, 115, 122, 124, 197, 200
Corvin, R. O., 39, 47
Courtney, Howard P., 86, 91
"covenant commitments," 79–80
Cremeens, Timothy, 16
Cross and the Switchblade, The (Wilkerson), 44
Crouch, Paul, 197
Cunningham, Loren, 83
Curtis Hotel, "shootout at," 82–83

Darby, John Nelson, 175
Daugherty, Billy Joe, 150, 182
De Celles, Dan, 87
De Celles, Paul, 79
Dirkschneider, Dale, 59
Discipline of the Pentecostal Holiness Church, 28
Dollar, Creflo, 112, 124
Drum, Woodard, 43
du Plessis, David, 69, 71, 72, 78, 79, 80, 83, 96, 101, 102
Duke, James, 119
Duran, Eduardo, 48
Duran, Raquel, 48
Durham, William, 22, 23

Edge, Hattie, 32
Edwards, Jonathan, 155–56
Edwards, Quinton, 172
Emmanuel College, 43, 44, 46, 48, 68, 75, 130, 193, 201
Eure, Carol, 55
Evans, Donald, 150
Evening Light Saints, 22
Ewing, Gene, 124
exorcisms (mass), 78
false teachings/movements, 28
Falwell, Jerry, 194
Farah, Chuck, 78
Father's Blessing, The (J. Arnott), 161
Federal Council of Churches, 33, 34
Fike, Doug, 99
Finished Work movement, 28, 33
Fischer, Balthasar, 70
"fivefold ministries," 35, 180
Fletcher, John, 175
Fletcher, Michael, 182
Flower, J. Roswell, 23, 34
Forbes, James, 93
Ford, Jane Massingbyrd, 68
Forrest, Tom, 101, 105, 111, 199
Fort Lauderdale Five, 78–79, 81, 89
  Oklahoma City meeting concerning, 83–84
  opposition to their leadership among Pentecostals, 82–83
Francescon, Luigi, 23, 180
Franklin, Benjamin, 119
Fredes, Alexia, 48
Freidzon, Claudio, 164
Frost, Robert, 82, 87, 89
Full Gospel Business Men's Fellowship International (FGBMFI), 16, 41, 58, 60, 102, 105, 111, 122
Fullam, Terry, 101
Fuller, Charles, 34
Fuller Theological Seminary, 181
  signs and wonders class at, 129–30
Fullness, 138–39

Gause, Hollis, 51
General Conference of the Pentecostal Holiness Church, 73–74
General Congress on the Holy Spirit and World Evangelization, 102, 108–12
  media coverage of, 112
  planning for, 102–5
  potential problems concerning, 105–8
  theme of, 103
George, Carl, 131
German Catholic Apostolic Church, 176

Ghezzi, Bert, 67, 199
Glencoe, 80–82, 84–85, 95, 96
"God is Restoring His People" (Martin), 86
Gospel of Wealth, The (Carnegie), 120
Grabe, Peter, 202
Grace, Marjorie, 199
Grace, Peter, 199
Graham, Billy, 41, 109, 121
Green, Charles, 98, 99, 103
Green, Michael, 109
Green, Samuel, 99, 147

Hagin, Kenneth, Jr., 115, 122–23
Hamilton, Carl, 39
Hanegraaff, Hank, 115
Hanson, Jane, 101, 105, 111
Harrell, Ed, 49
Hathaway, Alden, 110
Hawn, Robert, 86, 91
Hawtin, George, 35
Hayford, Jack, 148, 150–51, 181
healing crusades, 36–41
  salvation-healing crusades, 121, 123
Heflin, Ruth, 37
Heflin, Wallace, 37
Hill, E. V., 105, 109
Hill, Napoleon, 37, 122
Hill, Steve, 160, 163–64, 165, 166
Hinn, Benny, 115, 124, 203
Holiness movement. *See* Azusa Street Revival
Holiness Pentecostal Movement in the United States, The (Vinson Synan), 16, 44
Holy Spirit, the, 24–25, 35, 56–67, 69, 198
  actualization of the gifts of, 128
  baptism in, 45, 56, 58, 61, 66, 69, 72, 75, 99, 112, 135, 164, 177
  gifts of, 127, 128, 131, 175–76
  manifestations of at revival meetings, 158, 159, 164
  See also speaking in tongues, as evidence of baptism in the Holy Spirit
Hoover, Willis C., 23, 180

Howell, Paul, 73–74
Hromas, Bobbie, 112
Hunter, Harold D., 153
Hybels, Bill, 182

Ignite Church, 166, 167–68, 169
India, 203
Innocent IV (pope), 118
Irish, Chuck, 99
Irving, Edward, 175–76
Irving, Howard, 56, 78, 85
Islamic fundamentalism, 191–93

Jackson, Jim, 103
Jackson, Wilbur, 99
Jacobs, Sam, 199
Jakes, T. D., 124
Jensen, Jerry, 105
Jernigan, Dennis, 133–34
Jesus Movement, 44–46, 129
Jesus Only (Oneness) movement, 28, 33, 38
Jesus Persons, 44
John Paul II (pope), 198
Jones, O. T., 148

Kansas City charismatic conference, 90–94
  calls for a Kansas City II conference, 95–96
  media coverage of, 93–94
  planning for, 86–90
Kellar, Nancy, 99, 199
Kendrick, Klaud, 51
Kenyon, E. W., 122
Kerr, Cecil, 73
Kerr, Myrtle, 73
Kilpatrick, Brenda, 163
Kilpatrick, John, 163, 165
Kim, David, 182
Knapp, Martin Wells, 22
Koch, Roy, 85
Koontz, Linda, 102
Kuhlman, Kathryn, 57, 197
Kumuyi, William, 182

Lake, John G., 22, 23
Lamberth, Roy, 86
Latter Rain Movement, 33, 35–36, 37, 171–72, 180–81
Lewis, Brad, 16
Liardon, Roberts, 182
Lindvall, Terry, 201
Litwiller, Nelson, 85, 86, 92, 95–96, 99, 102

Long, Eddie, 124
Look Out! The Pentecostals Are Coming (Wagner), 130
Lovelace, Richard, 137
Lovett, Leonard, 150, 153
Luther, Martin, 118

Mahoney, Ralph, 80, 82, 83
Mainse, David, 110
Malachuk, Dan, 83
Mandela, Nelson, 191
Mani of Persia, 174
manifested sons, 35
Mansfield, Patti Gallagher, 91
Marion Apostolic Center, 80, 81
Marshall, Catherine, 92
Martin, Ralph, 67, 86, 91, 93
Mason, Charles H., 23, 145
McDonald, George, 175
McDonald, James, 175
McDonnell, Kilian, 51, 63, 66, 69, 81, 85, 128
McGavran, Donald, 120, 121, 200
McKinney, Joseph, 199
McNutt, Francis, 80, 84, 91
McTernan, John, 70, 72
megachurches (bell churches), 199–200
Melilli, Jerry, 106
Melodyland Christian Center, 57–58
Melodyland School of Theology, 57, 58
Melton, T. A., 37, 207n3
"Memphis Miracle," 149–54
Mendelsohn, Bob, 99
Menzies, William, 50, 51
Methodist charismatics, 90
Meyer, Joyce, 112, 124, 197
Middlebrook, Samuel, 150
Miller, Sandy, 160
Miracle of Seed Faith, The (Roberts), 122
miracles, of healing, 25
Mirley, Herb, 59
Mishler, Dick, 90
Mohammad the prophet, 174
Montague, George, 128
Montgomery, G. H., 39
Montgomery, Horace, 43
Moore, David, 16
Moore, Gary, 85, 99
Moore, Oscar, 39, 40
Mora, Gamalier, 48

Mormons (Church of Jesus Christ of Latter-day Saints), 174
church governance organization, 178–79
missionary work of, 179
origins of, 177–78
practice of plural marriage by, 178
Mount Olive Pentecostal Holiness Church, 42
Mouw, Richard, 66
Muehlen, Heribert, 70
Mumford, Bob, 79, 83, 86, 92, 105, 109
Muslims, 204
See also Islamic fundamentalism

National Association of Evangelicals (NAE), 34, 145
National Council of Churches (NCC), 33, 145
neo-charismatic movement, 138
Neo-Pentecostals, 54–57
growth of, 57–58
New Apostolic Churches, 181–82
New Apostolic Churches (Wagner), 182
New Apostolic Reformation, 169, 171–74, 181–83
critical reactions to, 183–86
New Covenant, 67, 69
New Orleans Leaders' Congress, 100–102
planning for, 99–100
See also General Congress on the Holy Spirit and World Evangelization
New Wine, 79
Ngugi, Simon, 112
Nickel, Thomas, 109
North American Renewal Services Committee (NARSC), 98, 134, 146, 147
Nunes, Winston, 85

Obama, Barack Hussein, 191
O'Brien, Veronica, 199
O'Connor, Edward, 67–68
Old Time Power, The (Vinson Synan), 74
On the Crest of the Wave: Becoming a World Christian (Wagner), 132
Open Bible Standard Churches, 34
Oral Roberts University, 41
Osborn, Tommy Lee, 41, 196
Osborn, Tommy Lee, Jr., 41
Osteen, Joel, 124
Osterberg, Arthur, 22
Oyedepo, David, 114, 123, 182

Pagard, Ken, 86
Paloma, Margaret, 162–63
Parham, Charles Fox, 20, 21, 91, 112, 179–80
Parham, Pauline, 91
Parks, Joseph, 44
Patterson, Gilbert, 148, 150
Patterson, J. O., 92, 147
Paul, Harold, 39
Pentecostal and Charismatic Churches of North America (PCCNA), 153–54
Pentecostal Churches of North America (PCNA), 152
Pentecostal Evangel, 50
Pentecostal Fellowship of North America (PFNA), 34–35, 146, 148–49
integration of, 151
Pentecostal Holiness Church, 16, 20, 26, 34, 37, 39, 131, 142, 180
rejection of the Latter Rain Movement, 36
types of apostles recognized by, 184–85
"Pentecostal Jim Crowism," 147
Pentecostal Movement in the Catholic Church, The (O'Connor), 68
Pentecostal revival, 127
Pentecostal World Conference, 63
Pentecostalism, 21, 23–24, 53–54, 133, 179, 183
in Africa, 123, 138, 203
in the American South, 23
classical Pentecostal movement, 9, 24, 133, 138, 160, 183
evangelicalization of, 34
growth of, 194–96
in New York City, 196
in South America, 138
Pentecostals, 185, 194, 203
burned out Pentecostals, 159
Catholic Pentecostals, 198
classical Pentecostals, 13, 36–37, 61, 85, 86, 88, 97, 135, 203
initial view of television, 197
Oneness Pentecostals, 33, 151
Pentecostal apostles, 179–81, 184–85
views on alcohol and tobacco use, 66–67
Pike, Garnet, 51
Pinchbeck, Dean, 42
Pinnock, Clark, 162
positive confession, 122
Price, Fred, 112, 124
Prince, Derek, 61, 78, 83, 84
prosperity gospel, 113–14
historical roots of, 117–18
post–World War II prosperity teachings, 121–23
prosperity televangelists, 124–26
Protestant gospel of wealth in the gilded age, 118–20
redemption and life, concept of, 120–21
three gospel messages concerning, 116–17
worldwide spread of, 114–15
Protestant ethic, the, 119

race/racial issues, in American church history, 144–46
and the Azusa Street Revival, 145
conversion of slaves to Christianity, 144
divisions along racial lines in Pentecostal churches, 145–46
rise of black churches, 144
See also racial unity, in the Pentecostal charismatic movement
"Racial Reconciliation Manifesto," 153
racial unity, in the Pentecostal charismatic movement, 146–47
architects of the unity process, 148–49
See also "Memphis Miracle"
Ramirez, Eugenio, 48

Ranaghan, Dorothy, 67, 110, 199
Ranaghan, Kevin, 67, 79, 81, 83, 84, 85, 86, 87, 91, 97, 99, 100, 110, 147, 199
Rapture of the Church, the, 27–28, 33, 176, 181, 189, 192
Reagan, Ronald, 194
rebaptizing, of charismatics, 78
Redeemed Christian Church of God, 115, 123, 182
Reems, Earnestine, 112
Regent University, 201–2
  desegregation of, 191
Renewal Theology (J. R. Williams), 128
revivals/spiritual awakenings, 155
  First Great Awakening, 155–56
  Fourth Great Awakening, 157
  Lakeland Revival, 166–69
  Laughing Revivals, 158
  Second Great Awakening, 156
  Third Great Awakening, 156–57
  See also Brownsville Revival; Jesus Movement; Latter Rain Movement; Toronto Blessing revival
Revolution in Rome (Wells and Woodbridge), 71
Richardson, Carl, 110
Robeck, Cecil M., 150, 153
Roberts, Evelyn, 26
Roberts, Oral, 26–27, 32, 37–38, 40, 101–2, 114, 115, 123, 124, 196, 197, 200, 201
  controversy concerning his ministry, 39–40
  and the gospel of prosperity, 121–22
Robertson, Pat, 79, 82, 83, 100, 106, 125, 164, 194, 197, 202
Robinson, Ras, 138
Roman Catholics, 59, 60, 61, 85, 89, 90, 95, 110, 111, 166, 173, 198, 204
  Catholic charismatics, 203
  Catholic Neo-Pentecostals, 63–65
  Catholic Pentecostal Dialogue meeting (Rome), 69–73
  wealth of the Catholic Church, 117–18
Rumsey, Mary, 23
Russellism, 28

salvation, 23, 25, 61, 110, 117, 123, 126, 135
sanctification, 23, 25, 28, 29, 33, 37, 61
Sawyer, Diane, 197
Scanlan, Mike, 93
Schihl, Bob, 201
Schuler, Robert, 105, 197
segregation, 28–29
Seymour, William J., 20, 21–22, 29, 145, 179
Shakarian, Demos, 41, 79, 82, 83, 102, 111, 122
Sheen, Fulton, 197
Shepherd's Conferences, 80, 81–82
Shetler, Joanne, 110
Simpson, Charles, 78, 83
Sklorenko, David, 98, 104, 107, 199
slavery, 144
Sloan, William, 54
Smith, Chuck, 45–46, 129, 130
Smith, Joseph, 177–78
social Darwinism, 120
social gospel, 116, 200
Society for Pentecostal Studies (SPS), 49–52, 63, 146
Southwestern Pentecostal Holiness College, 39–40
speaking in tongues, 35, 36, 54, 56, 61, 175, 177–78
  as evidence of baptism in the Holy Spirit, 127, 128, 133, 134–35
  singing in the Spirit, 133, 157
Spencer, Carleton, 86
Spittler, Russell, 51
Sproull, O. E., 39
Stanley, Charles, 197
Stapleton, Ruth Carter, 91
Steele, Collins, 39
Stephanau, Eusebius, 58
Stern, David, 87
Stone, Barton, 156
Stoop, Vernon, 90, 97, 99, 103
Strader, Karl, 85, 99, 166, 172
Strader, Steve, 166, 167, 168–69
Suenens, Joseph, 80, 92, 198, 199
Sullivan, Francis, 70
Swaggart, Jimmy, 106, 197
Synan, Carol Lee, 16, 43
Synan, Lindsay, 31, 32, 37
Synan, Madeline, 32
Synan, Mary Carol, 43
Synan, Maurine, 32
Synan, Vernon, 32, 40
Synan, Vinson, 24–29, 113–14, 204–6
  academic and ministerial career of, 29–30, 39, 40, 75, 200–202
  changes in the charismatic world during his lifetime, 198–99
  changes in the Pentecostal world during his lifetime, 194–97
  changes in the political world during his lifetime, 188–94
  as a child during World War II, 188–89
  as a child in a segregated community, 141–42, 190–91
  education of, 30, 39, 40, 42–44, 187–88, 201
  election as chairman of the Charismatic Concerns Committee, 97
  experiences in communist Russia, 190
  experiences with megachurches (bell churches), 199–200
  initial opinion of Catholics, 63–64
  keynote speech of at the General Congress on the Holy Spirit and World Evangelization, 108
  musicianship in his family, 32
  participation in the "Memphis Miracle," 149–50, 152
  as a pastor, 42–43
  and Pentecostal Catholics, 64–75, 199
  predictions for the future of Pentecostal and charismatic movements, 202–4

reactions to the New Apostolic Movement, 183–86
speaking of on the charismatic circuit, 58–61, 107–8, 163, 199
talk of on the three streams, 91
view of the 9/11 attacks, 192
work of with troubled youth, 46–47

Taylor, Jack, 138
televangelists, 124–26, 197
Think and Grow Rich (N. Hill), 37, 122
Third Wave of the Spirit movement, 132
future of, 137–39
major tenets of, 132–33
in New Orleans, 135–37
Thompson, Ray, 90
three streams. *See* charismatic renewal, three streams of
Tilton, Bob, 124
Tomlinson, A. J., 49
Toronto Blessing revival (Toronto Airport Vineyard Church), 158–63, 164–65, 169
formation of the Toronto Airport Christian Fellowship, 162
liturgy used in, 159
media coverage of, 160
origins of, 158–59
Trask, Thomas, 152
Turner, William, 150
Twelftree, Graham, 202
Tyson, Tommy, 198

Under His Banner (Vinson Synan), 41
Understanding Church Growth (McGavran), 120
Underwood, Bernard, 147, 148
United Pentecostal Church, 38

Vaagenes, Morris, 85, 99
Vasquez, Isabella, 48
Vasquez, Javier, 47, 48, 199, 205
Vasquez, Jorge, 48
Vingren, Gunnar, 23
Von Trapp, Maria, 92
Voronaev, Ivan, 23, 180

Wagner, C. Peter, 129–31, 134, 135, 136–37, 181, 183, 184
Walker, "Little David," 36
Walker, Paul, 152
Walker, Robert, 129–30
Ward, Horace, 49, 50
Wehmeyer, Peggy, 197
Weiner, Bob, 103, 110
Wesley, John, 175
Western Hills Baptist Church, 133–34
Whetstone, Ross, 59, 85, 86, 90, 99
White, Paula, 124, 197
White, Randy, 197
Whitefield, George, 156
Whitten, Clark, 138
"Who Are the Modern Apostles?" (Vinson Synan), 173
Whyte, Maxwell, 85
Wigglesworth, Smith, 167
Wilkerson, David, 44, 164
Wilkerson, Ralph, 57, 82
Williams, Floyd, 74
Williams, J. Rodman, 57, 58, 70, 72, 81, 128
Williams, Jo, 58
Wimber, Carol, 130
Wimber, John, 101, 111, 129–31, 135, 136, 137–38, 158
conflicts with John Arnott, 161–62
healing power of, 136
Women's Aglow, 105, 111
Word of Faith Movement, 114, 123. *See also* prosperity gospel
World Council of Churches (WCC), 33, 34
World Pentecostal Conference, 40, 51
Wyatt, Thomas, 196

Yale University, 54–55
Yocum, Bruce, 67, 93
Yoido Full Gospel Church, 114
Yong, Amos, 202
Young, Brigham, 178
Your Spiritual Gifts Can Help Your Church Grow (Wagner), 131

Zimmerman, Thomas, 51, 92

Vinson Synan, Dean Emeritus of the School of Divinity at Regent University in Virginia Beach, Virginia, received his Ph.D. in American history in 1967 from the University of Georgia. In 1970 he cofounded the Society for Pentecostal Studies, which has given institutional shape to Pentecostal research. Over the years, Dr. Synan has published numerous scholarly and popular articles, essays and books on various Pentecostal and charismatic themes.

His *Holiness-Pentecostal Movement*, published in 1971, was one of the few early scholarly treatments of Pentecostalism and is still a significant work on the origins of American Pentecostalism. His *Old-Time Power* (1973) is a history of the Pentecostal Holiness Church, and the more popularly written *In The Latter Days* (1984) and *The Twentieth-Century Pentecostal Explosion* (1987) are surveys of the Pentecostal and charismatic movements. He has also published a brief descriptive account of the Full Gospel Business Men's Fellowship, *Under His Banner* (1992), and *The Spirit Said "Grow"* (Fuller Church Growth Lectures, 1990). His newest major book, *Century of the Holy Spirit* (2001), is a historical summary of the major streams of Pentecostal and charismatic renewal. Another book of personal testimonies, *Voices of Pentecost*, appeared in May, 2003.

An ordained minister in the Pentecostal Holiness Church, Dr. Synan has founded and pastored four churches and has held various denominational offices. He has participated in the International Roman Catholic-Pentecostal Dialogue, and has served as chairman of several large Congresses on the Holy Spirit and World Evangelization.